PRAISE FOR THE FIRST EDITION

"A well-researched and balanced book about one of the great issues of our time."
South China Morning Post

"An exemplary introduction not only to China's ecological crisis, but also to the analytic tools that might help us to understand and approach it constructively."
China Dialogue

"This revolutionary book could be one of the key environmental texts of our age."
Times Higher Education

"A well-written book with an astonishingly captivating authorial voice. Fascinating, thoughtful and topical."
International Affairs

"An excellent introduction to China's mounting environmental challenges and the prospects for change - relevant for students, young researchers and the general public."
China Journal

"A concise and illuminating book."
Financial Times

"Shapiro should be applauded for leveraging her unusual sensitivity to and superb knowledge of China's historical and cultural complexities to generate a fascinating account of the monumental environmental changes currently under way in that country."
Perspectives on Politics

"An excellent textbook, which I would recommend to any reader interested in a well-written and balanced account of the toll rapid economic growth has taken on China's environment."
The Copenhagen Journal of Asian Studies

"A valuable source for covering the environment in Chinese politics courses, and an up-to-date text for the political sections of anthropology and geography courses that cover Chinese environmental problems."
China Quarterly

CHINA'S ENVIRONMENTAL CHALLENGES

CHINA'S ENVIRONMENTAL CHALLENGES

Second Edition

Judith Shapiro

polity

First edition published in 2012 by Polity Press
This edition published in 2016 by Polity Press

Polity Press
65 Bridge Street
Cambridge CB2 1UR, UK

Polity Press
350 Main Street
Malden, MA 02148, USA

ISBN-13: 978-0-7456-9863-2
ISBN-13: 978-0-7456-9864-9(pb)

A catalogue record for this book is available from the British Library.

Library of Congress Cataloging-in-Publication Data

Shapiro, Judith.
   China's environmental challenges / Judith Shapiro. – Second edition.
      pages cm – (China today)
   Includes bibliographical references and index.
   ISBN 978-0-7456-9863-2 (Hardback) – ISBN 978-0-7456-9864-9 (Paperback)
1. Environmental management–China.   2. Environmental management–China–
History.   3. Environmental policy–China–Citizen participation.   4. Sustainable development–
China.   5. China–Environmental conditions.   I. Title.
   GE320.C6.S53 2016
   333.70951–dc23

                                    2015020717

Typeset in 11.5 on 15 pt Adobe Jenson Pro
by Toppan Best-set Premedia Limited
Printed and bound in Great Britain by MPG Books Group Limited, Bodmin, Cornwall

For further information on Polity, visit our website: www.politybooks.com

Contents

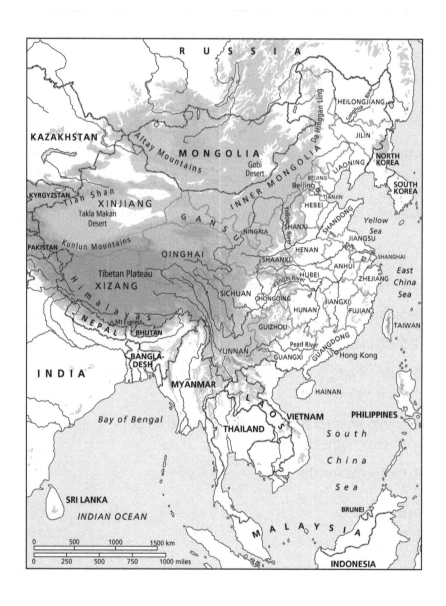

Chronology ─────────────────────

1894–95	First Sino-Japanese War
1911	Fall of the Qing dynasty
1912	Republic of China established under Sun Yat-sen
1927	Split between Nationalists (KMT) and Communists (CCP); civil war begins
1931	Central China floods kill millions
1934–1935	CCP under Mao Zedong evades KMT in Long March
December 1937	Nanjing Massacre
1937–1945	Second Sino-Japanese War
1945–1949	Civil war between KMT and CCP resumes
October 1949	KMT retreats to Taiwan; Mao founds People's Republic of China (PRC)
1950–1953	Korean War
1953–1957	First Five-Year Plan; PRC adopts Soviet-style economic planning
1954	First constitution of the PRC and first meeting of the National People's Congress
1956–1957	Hundred Flowers Movement, a brief period of open political debate
1957	Anti-Rightist Movement, a period of repression
1958–1960	Great Leap Forward, an effort to transform China through rapid industrialization and collectivization

March 1959	Tibetan uprising in Lhasa; Dalai Lama flees to India
1959–1961	Three Hard Years, widespread famine with tens of millions of deaths
Early 1960s	Sino-Soviet split
1962	Sino-Indian War
October 1964	First PRC atomic bomb detonation
1966–1976	Great Proletarian Cultural Revolution; Mao reasserts power
February 1972	President Richard Nixon visits China; Shanghai Communiqué pledges to normalize U.S.–China relations
June 1972	United Nations Conference on the Human Environment held in Stockholm
July 1976	Tangshan earthquake kills hundreds of thousands
September 1976	Death of Mao Zedong
October 1976	Ultra-Leftist Gang of Four arrested and sentenced
December 1978	Deng Xiaoping assumes power; launches Four Modernizations and economic reforms
1978	One-child family planning policy introduced
1979	U.S. and China establish formal diplomatic ties
1979	PRC invades Vietnam
January 1981	PRC ratifies 1973 Convention on International Trade in Endangered Species (CITES)
1982	Census reports PRC population at more than one billion
December 1984	Sino-British Joint Declaration agrees to return Hong Kong to China in 1997
1989	Tiananmen Square protests culminate in June 4 military crackdown

June 1991	PRC ratifies 1987 Montreal Protocol on Substances that Deplete the Ozone Layer
December 1991	PRC ratifies 1989 Basel Convention on the Control of Transboundary Movements of Hazardous Wastes and Their Disposal
April 1992	National People's Congress formally approves Three Gorges Dam
June 1992	United Nations Conference on Environment and Development held in Rio
1992	Deng Xiaoping's Southern Inspection Tour re-energizes economic reforms
1993–2002	Jiang Zemin becomes president of PRC, continues economic growth agenda
1998	Yangzi River floods kill thousands, leave millions homeless, prompt logging ban
March 1998	State Environmental Protection Administration (SEPA) created
November 2001	WTO accepts China as member
August 2002	World Summit on Sustainable Development held in Johannesburg; PRC ratifies 1997 Kyoto Protocol to the United Nations Framework Convention on Climate Change
2003–2013	Hu Jintao is president of PRC
2002–2003	SARS outbreak
2006	PRC supplants U.S. as largest gross CO_2 emitter
March 2008	State Environmental Protection Administration upgraded to Ministry of Environmental Protection
May 2008	Sichuan earthquake kills tens of thousands
August 2008	Summer Olympic Games in Beijing
2009	Three Gorges Dam major construction complete

2012	Xi Jinping appointed General-Secretary of the CCP (and President of PRC from 2013)
2013–2014	Multiple "Airpocalypse" pollution events in Beijing
December 2013	South-North Water Transfer East route opens
November 2014	"APEC Blue" summit and new US-China climate change commitments
December 2014	South-North Water Transfer Middle route opens
2015	Stringent new environmental laws come into effect; "Under the Dome" documentary rivets China; Huge chemical explosions hit the Chinese port city of Tianjin

Preface

I first visited the People's Republic of China in the summer of 1977. United States–China relations had not yet been normalized, Mao Zedong had been dead less than a year, and political posters plastered everywhere showed the Chairman lying on his sickbed with his chosen successor Hua Guofeng at his side, saying "With You in Charge, I am at Ease." Hua would only hold power until December 1978. A reformist government followed under the leadership of Deng Xiaoping, who returned from political exile and persecution to revolutionize China as profoundly as Mao did in 1949 when the Chinese Communist Party's army defeated Chiang Kai-shek's Nationalist Kuomintang (KMT) and drove it and its followers to Taiwan. Little did I know then, at the age of 24, that the parades and celebrations I witnessed in Shanghai marked the beginning of Deng's political rehabilitation. Nor did I understand that this political "opening" was about to transform China, the world, and also my own life, providing me with the opportunity to be among the first 40 Americans to teach English there, along with a few resident foreign Maoists who had managed to survive the turmoil of the Cultural Revolution.

China had been profoundly shut away from most of the outside world since the Sino-Soviet split in the early 1960s. What the West knew about the Mao years was limited largely to interviews with refugees conducted by scholars and government officials in Hong Kong, and glowing reports from left-wing "friends of China." When I was at university and graduate school in the 1970s, the United States was reeling from the unpopular Vietnam War. Many American young people were highly critical of the U.S. government and skeptical of its claims that our traditional enemies, China among them, could possibly be as bad as claimed. We knew vaguely about "people's communes," which sounded fascinating at a time when our domestic counter-culture movement was also experimenting with collective living. We also knew that in China it was said that "Women Hold Up Half the Sky," a compelling slogan for Western feminists who were expanding their intellectual, political, and personal influence and becoming a truly popular women's movement. Through "ping-pong diplomacy," or friendly sports matches intended to break down political barriers, and the limited cultural exchanges that followed the famous 1972 Nixon and Kissinger visit, we caught televised performances by the fantastic Shanghai acrobats, whose back-bending female contortionists could stack bowls on their heads with their feet while standing on their forearms, and whose male gymnasts could create tableaux of 20 figures balanced on a single circling bicycle. We admired naïve and charming peasant paintings that showed nets full of golden carp and fields of abundant harvests, with red-cheeked girls portrayed as members of the "Worker, Peasant, Soldier" proletariat. In retrospect, our romanticism was at best untutored and at worst dangerous. Nonetheless, it was the reason for my determination to learn Chinese, which I began studying in my sophomore year at Princeton, and to go to China to live.

I might have been more sensitive to signs that not everything was as rosy as I hoped, during my first visit in the summer of 1977. My organized group tour consisted of members of the U.S.–China People's Friendship Association, a populist organization intended to build people-to-people ties at a time when our governments were at loggerheads. At one point, we were traveling by overnight train from Beijing to Xi'an when the guide assigned to spend two weeks with us, a kindly middle-aged lady, returned from the train platform after a ten-minute stop, weeping profoundly. She was sharing a sleeping compartment with me and I asked what was wrong. She told the story of her beloved son who had been "sent down" from his home to the rural countryside to "learn from" the peasants. She had just seen him for the first time since he left home ten years earlier. She explained that the residence card system, which included everyone in China, kept him in exile. His residence card, or *hukou*, had been transferred to the countryside, keeping him trapped there; he would be unable to obtain ration coupons to buy rice, cooking oil, vegetables, clothing, and other life necessities anywhere else. She missed him terribly.

Also on that trip, an overseas Chinese woman in our group made every effort to contact her relatives and was finally allowed to glimpse them for a few moments. In the company of Party handlers, they were unable to speak freely and she was unable to discover what had happened to them during the Cultural Revolution. Their gaunt appearance and fearful demeanor made her profoundly worried.

However, instead of paying attention to these warning signals, I became more enamored than ever of a country whose people appeared strong and slim, warmly hospitable, and eager for our help. The women wore the same clothing as the men: blue or green pants and simple white shirts. They wore their hair in long braids or short bobs; they used no makeup, and indeed, there was none for sale. The men had brushy haircuts, bad teeth, and wonderfully winning smiles. The entire country seemed to rely on bicycles for transportation; automobiles were few, and reserved for "distinguished guests" like ourselves or for high-ranking Party officials. The Chinese were clearly thrilled we were visiting – everywhere we drew huge, curious, friendly crowds. Foreigners unlucky enough to be tall or to have blond or red hair were mobbed. The Chinese begged us to come back and help them to develop. Profoundly moved, I was determined to try to make a contribution.

When in early 1979 the phone call came from the Chinese Embassy telling me I had been selected to teach English in Hunan Province, I was a Masters degree student in Asian Studies at the University of California, Berkeley. With almost six years of Chinese language training and blessed with short stature and dark hair to help me blend into local crowds, I was as well equipped as any American might have been for the experiences that lay ahead. In retrospect, I was totally unprepared for the shocking stories I heard once I arrived and the moving events I experienced. In the course of those early two-and-a-half years of life in China, I made deep and often dangerous friendships (foreigners were still widely viewed as spies), traveled to numerous places where no foreigner had been, witnessed the struggles of a country recovering from a prolonged nightmare, and found my own writer's voice as someone who could bear witness to the suffering of a people who had no other court of appeal.

Hunan Province was Chairman Mao's home province. As a result, Maoism ran deep. Ultra-leftist military men were entrenched in power at my university, Hunan Teachers' College, and they were not at all pleased to be sent a Western foreign teacher, even if (or perhaps especially since) her English was considered an essential tool of the modernization policy of the new government. The "foreign expert" was given a large apartment, by Chinese standards, and fitted with the only air conditioner on the campus. When I turned it on, the electricity in the whole college went out – I refrained from using it. I was assigned a Party handler, a charming young woman teacher whose only duty was to spend every possible moment monitoring my activities. I fought back against her smothering attention vigorously, with eventual success. After several months she was allowed to return to her teaching assignments and instead I was placed under the charge of a genial retired army officer with a second-grade education (the military was still controlling the universities), who let me do as I pleased. I fought also for the right to ride a bicycle instead of being chauffeured in one of the only three cars in the campus garage (what if the foreigner had an accident or went somewhere off limits?) and to practice my passionate hobby, ballet, with the local song and dance troupe, who spoke of their affection for the Russian teachers who had been forced home after relations collapsed with the 1960 Sino-Soviet Split. I also fought for the right to attend the required weekly political study sessions for faculty, only to feel confused by the ill-concealed hatred that the professors displayed for the leaders, who sat in front of the room reading Party directives aloud from the official newspapers. The professors whispered loudly, knitted, spat, and showed their disdain; this was hardly what I expected.

But my political education began in earnest when I was at last permitted to teach the students. In my first months, I was considered too precious a commodity to share with anyone but the professors, many of whom were elderly former Russian teachers attempting to retool for the country's modernization drive. However, in 1977 the first examinations for university entrance had been held since before the ultra-leftist Cultural Revolution began in 1966. The students were brilliant; no professor was qualified to teach them because most English instructors had built their careers on obscure points of grammar or laborious translations of the classics (one had even achieved professorship for his translations of the poems of Chairman Mao), and at last the top students were put under my tutelage. Many of them were my age, in their mid-twenties, and had studied English in secret, often while in the countryside where they had been sent, like my former tour guide's son, to "learn from" the peasants. Such studying was highly dangerous; during the Cultural Revolution you could lose your life for listening to the Voice of America or the BBC. Yet these students, confused and embittered by the sacrifices they had made seemingly for naught, risked everything to ask questions about the outside world and about the regime under which they grew up and by which they felt misled, tricked, and exploited. They gradually started to share their stories with me, through class essays and friendships. Ironically, they often trusted me, an outsider, far more than they trusted each other, for every class had its student spies who would report what was said in order to gain their own political advancement.

From my students, I began to learn the grassroots perspective on the history of China after Mao came to power. They recalled how they were told that they were the luckiest people in the world to be born after 1949 into China's new socialist paradise. They told of the 1956–1957 Hundred Flowers Movement, a brief few months when people were encouraged to criticize the regime so as to improve it, and of the 1957 Anti-Rightist Movement which followed immediately after, when many of China's most brilliant and outspoken intellectuals, scientists, and political leaders were labeled as Rightists, silenced, imprisoned, exiled, and even executed. Although my students were children at the time, some had lost parents to politically induced divorce or persecution, and they themselves had been viewed as politically suspect as a result. They also knew about famous intellectuals, writers, and artists who were denounced as Rightists, silenced, and sent into exile in the countryside, never again to publish or resume their professional duties. They told me about the 1958–1960 Great Leap Forward, when China tried to catch up with industrialized nations through a great burst of social mobilization. Every "work unit," whether school, factory, hospital, or government institution, was organized to smelt steel in "backyard furnaces" in an effort to move China past its domineering "elder brother," the Soviet Union, and compete directly with developed Western countries in industrial output and modernization. Children and adults alike killed rats, lice, sparrows, and mosquitoes, the so-called Four Pests; farmers were induced to conduct agricultural experiments in deep plowing and close planting intended to yield one bumper harvest after the next. The "Three Hard Years" arrived immediately, from 1959 to 1961, after officials neglected the harvest, natural disasters arrived, and grain rotted in the fields. This was one of the most severe human-created famines in history, with somewhere around 30 million deaths that would not otherwise have occurred. My students told me about eating bark and gathering bitter weeds, about grandparents who starved while giving food to their children and grandchildren. Even those from big cities remembered terrible shortages. At the time, I was not attuned to the story of the deforestation that fueled the backyard furnaces, or to thinking of the great famine as a great ecological collapse, but, of course, that is what it was. Both were expressions of Mao's attempt to conquer nature.

I also heard from my students about the turmoil of the 1966–1976 Cultural Revolution. Many of them had been swept into the competitive frenzy to protect Mao against his purported enemies and joined the Red Guards, only to be manipulated into violent factional struggle against each other and against rival Red Guard groups from other universities and work units. They told of verbally and physically attacking and humiliating teachers and Party leaders, of putting up Big Character Posters drawn in large brushstrokes that enumerated the counter-revolutionary, reactionary, and revisionist crimes of the accused, of riding trains for free around the country to spread the revolution, of ritually recreating the 1934–1935 Long March by hiking arduously from one Red Army historical site to another, of humiliating religious leaders, writers, and artists for their so-called reactionary attachment to the Four Olds: old customs, culture, habits, and beliefs. They told me, too, of denouncing their own parents and siblings in an effort to be more "Red" and revolutionary than anyone else. What they did not then understand was that they were pawns in a power struggle at elite levels of political life. The protagonists included Mao's ultra-leftist radical wife Jiang Qing and her three close associates (later denounced as the Gang of Four), Mao himself, and a large cast of other central-level leaders who disagreed sharply on the political direction of the country. They also did not know that at provincial and local levels, the Cultural Revolution provided an opportunity for old rivals to settle scores. Even less were they able to reflect on their own role and responsibility for a culture of obedience, through which patronage and fealty could easily be manipulated into violent factionalism. Their impulse toward free expression, to travel throughout the country and spread revolution, and to challenge a repressive and authoritarian educational and political system, had been abused and manipulated by forces they did not understand.

Almost all of my students had been made to "volunteer" to resettle in the countryside after those few months of chaos and gratuitous violence. In early 1967, Mao sent the army into universities, middle schools, factories, and government offices in an effort to regain control, and there was nowhere to send young people when so many schools and factories were closed. Many of these "educated youth" were organized into military-style encampments and set to manual labor on China's frontiers, filling in wetlands and cutting down forests, attacking nature as they had attacked Mao's purported enemies in the Party.

During the early post-Mao years of university life, I also worked with professors who had returned from the countryside, having been subjected to so many self-criticism sessions that they were terrified of speaking and often shielded their mouths with their hands. I met students whose only exposure to literature was from the Marxist left, whose only intellectual life had been political study in which they were made to memorize Party texts and repeat slogans. Their wicked sense of humor included using such slogans ironically in daily speech. I felt a great responsibility to provide a bridge to the world of ideas and culture. My students had never heard of Freud or the notion of the unconscious; the Beatles and Rolling Stones were unknown; the Three Mile Island nuclear meltdown was not mentioned in their newspapers when it occurred soon after my arrival in March 1979. Romantic love was still considered dangerous, if not counterrevolutionary – if a boy wrote a letter to a girl and they went for a walk together, it was tantamount to engagement and marriage. My library of foreign books, some sent ahead, some provided by the U.S. Embassy, and many cadged from generous foreign tourists, was treated as a treasure trove.

In this atmosphere, I met and eventually married a young Chinese literature student, Liang Heng. To get permission for the marriage we had to appeal to "paramount leader" Deng Xiaoping himself. As we were courting, Liang Heng narrated his life story to me systematically in Chinese and I wrote it down in English before translating it back to him orally in Chinese; this process helped him come to terms with the political upheaval that had ripped his family apart even as it helped me to understand, on a visceral level, just how traumatic the Cultural Revolution had been for the Chinese people. We later published this memoir as *Son of the Revolution*. We emigrated to the U.S. after Liang Heng received his degree and I had been in China for nearly three years, but we continued to return frequently to China, writing additional books about China's reforms and the changes in intellectual life. Traveling widely, we chronicled China's growing freedoms and ongoing restraints, political repression, and limits on access to information. Our adventures in remote areas closed to foreigners often involved late-night knocks on the doors of fleabag hotels where we were staying; uniformed local Public Security Bureau officials demanded to see our passports and reprimanded us for being in "closed" areas. But we evaded the serious repression experienced by democracy activists, who were sometimes sent to prison or labor camps merely for their ideas or publications, because Liang Heng was by then a U.S. citizen. China was opening up and it was often enough to apologize for being in the wrong place and continue on our way the next day. Despite such constraints, the changes under Deng Xiaoping were astounding, and by comparison to life under Mao, Chinese society under the reforms was markedly better as people's standard of living began to improve and their intense fear to abate.

Economic freedoms far outpaced political ones. In the countryside, the people's communes were disbanded and *de facto* private plots created. Systems of leasing land allowed specialized production and unleashed enterprise and innovation. In the cities, the "iron rice bowl," which guaranteed basic food and shelter for everyone in Chinese society no matter what the contribution of their labor, was "smashed." Efficiency became the order of the day as enterprises had to show they could be profitable or they were closed down. Large state-owned enterprises such as the big iron and steel mills were often exceptions, but even they were expected to create sideline businesses to stay afloat. Individual entrepreneurs began to flourish, especially among the children of high-ranking officials who often had access to commodities that were supposed to be under state control. A gray area, neither socialist nor capitalist, became a significant part of the economy. Success in life depended on connections and access to people who could help you "go through the back door" to obtain regulated or scarce goods and special permissions.

Even during the "golden decade" of increased personal freedoms from 1979 to 1989, educated Chinese spoke of a "crisis of confidence" in the Party and socialism, and some members of the central government tried to reform the political system to keep up with economic reforms. Impatient with the slow pace of change, students and intellectuals in Beijing and other cities famously demonstrated beginning in April 1989, taking over Tiananmen Square for days. It was too much, too fast. Reformist leader and Party Secretary-General Zhao Ziyang begged the students to go home, foreseeing the massacre which arrived on June 4, killing hundreds if not thousands and setting back the reform effort. Zhao ended his days under house arrest for his role in promoting political liberalization and democracy.

In the aftermath, disillusioned with the state, many bright young people turned away from politics and focused on getting ahead economically. Business and computer schools flourished, and China came into its own as the world's manufacturing hub. Getting richer, in any way possible, became a shared national passion. Apparently, the Party would be allowed to stay in power as long as the people's living standards continued to rise. The dark side of this economic activity was, of course, resource depletion and industrial pollution, the subject of this book.

Meanwhile, back in the U.S., my own career turned to the study of global environmental politics. The marriage to Liang Heng had ended and I was looking for a new direction that would bring my China experiences together with my love of nature. Fascinated by the relationship between the intellectual and personal repressions I had witnessed and the way people were despoiling the planet, I returned to China in 1999 to teach at an agricultural university in Sichuan Province and collect material and interviews for a new book, *Mao's War against Nature*, which told personal stories about how the political repression of ordinary people was mirrored in an attack against nature. State-ordered transformation of human souls was often carried out through political campaigns marshalling collective labor to "Make mountains bow their heads, make rivers flow uphill," as a Mao-era poem expressed it. Mao's uneasiness with intellectuals allowed him to dismiss the most elementary of scientific principles and celebrate his notion, as a military general, that mobilizing the country into a vast army would allow him to defeat all enemies, both human and non-human.

As this book will show, the environmental problems of the post-Mao years have only become worse, with globalized free-market capitalism an equal if not greater driver of environmental degradation than the Stalinist-style state. Perhaps the root problem is not the economic system at all: both during and after Mao, limits on public participation and freedom of information have been great obstacles to the possibility that society collectively can make wise choices. Political repression, rapid change, and the state's willingness to reorder society for its own purposes have remained constant themes which put nature under assault. But as we will discover in our exploration of China's emerging civil society, which provides more "democratic space" for individuals to voice their concerns about the condition of the environment, there are signs that an environmental movement is now emerging to help protect endangered species and clean up the pollution created by socialist and capitalist cultures alike.

I eventually became a professor of global environmental politics at the School of International Service at American University in Washington, DC, where I teach the subject, using an interdisciplinary approach, to passionate graduate and undergraduate students who wish to find solutions to our environmental crisis. This book draws upon my efforts to clarify the many scholarly and political approaches to global environmental study; it pulls them together to shine a focused light on my primary passion, China. I hope that you, the readers, will enjoy the book and that you will find it helpful, inspiring, and not overly discouraging, even as it is a call to urgent action.

Acknowledgments and Note to the Second Edition

This book would not have been possible without the patient persuasion of my editor at Polity Press, Louise Knight, who convinced me to write it, and Neil de Cort and Pascal Porcheron, who shepherded it expertly and responsively through the publication process. Ian Tuttle copy-edited the manuscript with skill, sensitivity, and a keen eye. Many able readers were involved and I am in their debt, including Emily Yeh, Anna Brettell, Ken Conca, Mike Gelner, Gary Marcuse, Paul Wapner, and the eagle-eyed Jessica Blakely. Anonymous readers shaped the initial proposal and critiqued and improved the draft. Sikina Jinnah, Garrett Graddy, Ma Tianjie, Tim Kovach, Zhu Rong, and Christopher Carolin were also very helpful at critical stages. American University's School of International Service has been a wonderful base for scholarship and teaching, and I am most grateful to be here. I have learned much from my colleagues and students. For the initial book I was exceptionally fortunate to have the research assistance and editorial participation of Adam Jadhav, whose intelligent comments and willingness to delve deeply into the problems of a country that is not his beloved India were one of this project's most important assets. For the second edition I was equally fortunate: the book has benefited enormously from the experience and expertise, keen analytical mind, and collegiality of Gu Beibei from the Institute of Public and Environmental Affairs. I must also thank my ever-supportive husband Rick Shapiro, and my two cats, Binky and Scrushy, who responded to me much as they usually do, which was perhaps the greatest help of all.

The Second Edition has been thoroughly updated with the latest figures and trends, and it has been expanded in significant ways. It incorporates China's encouraging shift on climate change and "peak emissions" and its stringent new environmental laws, as well as the 2015 "Under the Dome" viral video phenomenon. The chapter on civil society has been reorganized and updated so as to highlight the many inventive and courageous strategies that Chinese environmental non-governmental organizations are using to shape public policy and behavior. Finally, there is an extensive new section on the global impacts of China's resources quest. I was greatly heartened by the initial book's warm reception and hope that the second edition will prove equally useful, both as a primer on China's environmental problems and as a roadmap toward solutions to our shared global challenges. I hope that it will encourage many more people to help shape one of the critical transformations of our time.

1 Introduction: The Big Picture

"Fires continue to burn in Tianjin days after explosions."
"One-fifth of China's Soil Contaminated."
"Polluted Farmland Leads to Chinese Food Security Fears."
"Amid Severe Drought, Chinese Government Admits Mistakes with Three Gorges Dam."
"Toxic Smog Threatens Millions of Chinese Lives."
"China Suspends New High-speed Rail Projects Following Crash."
"China Closes 'Toxic' Chemical Plant after Thousands Protest."
"Company Ordered to Halt Production after Dumping Toxic Waste."
"16,000 Dead Pigs Found in Chinese River, Threatening Shanghai's Water Supply."
"Thousands Riot in South China over Land Grab."
"Most of China's Coastal Waters Heavily Polluted."
"China's Hunger for Resources has Big Environmental Impact in Latin America."

This sampling of headlines, compiled from Chinese and international news stories from 2013 to 2015, reflects the breakneck changes in China's development, its global influence, and the enormity of the environmental problems that the country faces. How are we to make sense of the huge shift in China's position in the world? What does it mean for China's prospects for sustainable development? How does it affect the global environment? This book explores these questions.

China's huge environmental challenges are significant for us all. The choices the Chinese Communist Party, national government, and Chinese people are making influence not only the health and well-being of China but the very future of the planet. Environmental issues do not stop at state borders. China's air and water pollution, dam construction, and resource consumption have a profound impact around the world. What China does affects global climate change, ozone depletion, biodiversity loss, desertification, acid rain, commodity prices, fisheries, wildlife migrations, and a host of other environmental challenges. China's expanding economy, consumption of energy, and scarcity of arable land generate environmental problems in other countries such as Canada, where the environmentally fragile Alberta tar sands are being developed with the Chinese market in mind; Kenya, where vast areas of farmland are now owned by Chinese interests; and Myanmar (Burma), Vietnam, and Thailand, where local economies are being affected by China's construction of dams on the Salween and Mekong rivers. China's problems are interconnected with those of the rest of the planet.

China has become a major player in the international competition for resources, speeding up deforestation and land degradation around the globe. However, the huge size of China's environmental footprint is created, in part, by the export of the developed world's consumption costs: The raw materials that China extracts, not only at home but also overseas, often end up as products in stores in the developed world. The environmental degradation caused by China's resource extraction often takes place in distant countries, many in the developing world. The pollution generated during the manufacturing stage affects the Chinese people and the finished goods are often consumed in developed countries. When consumers are finished with the products, the trash is often re-exported to the developing world as part of the illegal trade in toxic waste. The Chinese state has positioned the country for explosive economic growth, and many Chinese are growing wealthy and reaping the benefits of China becoming a global manufacturing hub. Yet ordinary Chinese are bearing the brunt of global pollution, as they suffer the negative impacts of production in terms of reduced quality of life, prevalence of disease, and shortened life spans.

Here are a few striking examples of the transboundary implications of China's environmental challenges:

Particulate air pollution from China is regularly measured in California, Oregon, Washington State and Western Canada, and China is a major source of mercury deposition in the Western U.S., providing a striking reminder that a nation's environmental problems do not respect political boundaries. We know China is the source because Chinese air pollution has a high percentage of lead, and those measurements spike in Western North America in the spring when China's dust storms are most intense. The great size and intensity of these storms are caused in part by environmental mistakes made decades ago, during Mao's time, when northern grasslands were destroyed in an attempt to grow more wheat. But the sparse rainfall did not support grain production, crops died, and vast areas were reduced to desert. Now, when typhoons whip up massive dust storms over Inner Mongolia and Western China, debris can occasionally even be deposited as far away as Eastern Canada and Florida.

The dams China is building on the upper reaches of the Mekong River (in China, called the Lancang) and on the Salween River (in China, called the Nu) affect the water supply of the downriver states of Laos, Cambodia, Thailand, Vietnam, and Myanmar. Cambodians worry about the drying of lakes and the impact on fish, their primary protein source, while Vietnamese residents of the Delta are concerned about having enough water to support farming and other basic livelihoods. This dam-building activity is complicated by the fact that China (like Myanmar) is not a full member or treaty signatory but only a dialogue partner in the well-established Mekong River Commission; it is thus less likely to be bound by collective decisions. Upstream dam-building plans and activities in China on the rivers originating in the Tibetan Plateau and elsewhere in Western China could also threaten the water supplies of people in India, Nepal, Pakistan, Bangladesh, and Kazakhstan. As we see from this list, there are tensions over transboundary watercourses between China and almost all of its territorial neighbors.

Another international impact of China's environmental challenges involves the Chinese people's growing appetite for exotic meats, animal parts, and plants, which threatens rare and endangered species. Chinese gastronomic and medical traditions see consuming a species as a way of acquiring desirable characteristics like strength, prowess, and longevity. Chinese demand for body parts of rhinoceroses, tigers, bears, pangolins, and turtles, to name just a few creatures under siege, is felt in many other Asian countries and indeed throughout the world. Even in North America, American black bears are killed for their gall bladders, and wild plants like American ginseng root are poached from parks and protected areas and smuggled to the Chinese medicinal market. Sharks, whose fins are sliced off to make soup, are in decline throughout the world and captured from as far away as the Galapagos.

Since the 1998 Yangzi River floods, when China banned logging in the headwaters of its major rivers, China's import of exotic hardwoods from Indonesia, Myanmar, Cambodia, and other remaining tropical forests has increased dramatically. The ban increased pressure on some of the world's last remaining old-growth forests, in part to feed a market in furniture exported to the U.S. and other developed countries. The logging ban in China has also had an enormous effect on the forests of the Russian Far East, the last redoubt of the Siberian Tiger, and as far away as Canada, where the logging industry is enjoying a recovery thanks to its major new customer.

China has also overtaken the U.S. as the world's largest emitter of carbon dioxide (CO_2) and other greenhouse gasses. Together with other developing countries, China argues that its "survival emissions" should not be compared to the "luxury emissions" of developed countries, which have enjoyed the benefits of burning fossil fuels that put most of the carbon into the atmosphere and should rightfully bear the primary costs of saving the global atmospheric infrastructure which sustains life. This position affects the outcome of the ongoing global climate change negotiations. However, even in per capita terms China's emissions are rising dramatically, and pressure is mounting on China to modify its position that it should be treated as a developing country. Encouragingly, China is taking unilateral steps to reduce emissions intensity and increase the percentage of renewable resources in its energy mix. Most dramatically, as we shall see in detail later in the book, China has committed to peak its carbon emissions by 2030.

The rising middle class in China, as in India and other rapidly developing countries, is using more refrigerants and air conditioners, reversing some of the favorable movement toward repairing the thinning stratospheric ozone layer which protects the Earth from ultraviolet radiation. China, like other less-developed countries which signed the 1987 Montreal Protocol, had more time than developed ones to phase out ozone-depleting substances like CFCs (technically named chlorofluorocarbons and marketed as Freon), halons, and the agricultural fumigant methyl bromide, which is still used on strawberries and other crops. Although the phase-out period is over, CFC substitutes such as hydrofluorocarbons (HFCs) and hydrochlorofluorocarbons (HCFCs) are also ozone-depleting, if less so, and are also greenhouse gasses. Even in the best-case scenario, increased demand for such products in the developing world may undermine the world's most successful example of international cooperation on environmental issues.

Acid rain deposition from sulfur dioxide (SO_2) emissions, to which China is a major contributor, has destroyed forests in Japan and Korea.

This remains a sore point in diplomatic relations in Northeast Asia, with as much as half of the acid rain in the region coming from China's coal-fired power plants and automobile exhaust. As with carbon emissions, China is taking steps to reduce acid rain, with some success.

In the competition over power to exploit natural resources, the Chinese are asserting territorial maritime claims over the Spratly and Paracel Islands in the South China Sea. Multiple actors, including Vietnam, the Philippines, Malaysia, Brunei and Taiwan, also assert rights to oil and natural gas seabeds, fisheries, and shipping lanes. Fragile relationships in that region are unstable, and the United States' support for its traditional allies has created friction in the relationship between the U.S. and China.

Chinese international investment in oil, gas, and minerals, welcome as it may be to political elites overseas, fuels environmentally destructive extractive activities in places as far-flung as Peru, Ecuador, Liberia, Zambia, Sudan, and Iran. Chinese foreign aid programs often facilitate such extraction by carving roads into wilderness and across deserts, bringing development into fragile ecosystems and contributing to the current great wave of global species extinctions.

As fascinating and sobering as these examples may be, they cannot be understood fully without appreciating China's domestic political pressures, struggles, history, and culture. Thus, the primary focus of this book is on the domestic roots of some of these transnational challenges, for it is within China that much of the future of the planet will be decided. Conventional "realist" political analysis tends to see nation-states as unitary, power-seeking actors in an anarchic world, and does not uncover the complexity of China's political and social landscape. We need to recognize the multiplicity of actors who play a role in China's future and appreciate the country's geographic variety, regional disparities, and ethnic and cultural complexity, as well as the unique character of China's authoritarian political system, with its economic and social freedoms and contradictions. All of these factors will play a role in determining China's future environmental "footprint" and trans-national impacts. What are the implications of the fact that, as Joseph Kahn and Jim Yardley expressed it in an extensive *New York Times* series on China's environment, China is "Choking on Growth"? How will the Chinese navigate the challenges they are facing, and what dynamics affect their choices?

Before we begin to approach these enormous questions, here are just a few facts to illustrate the severity of China's environmental crisis. The World Bank has found that 20 of the world's 30 most polluted cities are in China, primarily because of heavy coal use, with Shanxi Province's coal-mining city Linfen the dirtiest. China's high economic growth rate – close to 10 percent per year between 2000 and 2014 – must be greatly discounted with the inclusion of environmental costs in lost work days, premature deaths, and pollution clean-up. In 2007, for example, the World Bank estimated the cost of Chinese pollution at 5.8% of GDP. Efforts by some government officials and think-tank scholars to create a reliable "Green Gross Domestic Product" calculation for China have stalled, in part because of the political sensitivity of the effort and the difficulty of obtaining reliable statistics.

Air pollution is a huge challenge. The problem was made famous by the attention to poor air quality in the capital during the lead-up to the 2008 Beijing Olympics, but it is sometimes even more serious in other parts of the country. The World Resources Institute (1999) found that total suspended particulates (TSP) and SO_2, both produced by burning coal, far exceed World Health Organization guidelines in the majority of Chinese cities. Indeed, life expectancy in Northern China is widely known to be more than 5.5 years shorter than that in the South due to long-term exposure to air pollution caused by heavy coal burning. In October 2013 the 10-million-resident city of Harbin was shut down for days because air pollution particulates were 40 times the level considered safe by the WHO, and vehicle drivers simply could not see. The term "airpocalypse" was used frequently in 2013 and 2014 to describe crippling levels of smog in Beijing. Lung diseases such as tuberculosis and cancer are so prevalent that Chinese "cancer villages," in which cancer death rates due to air and water pollution are far above the national average, are well documented. By 2010, the media and Internet had drawn attention to 459 cancer villages distributed across 29 of China's 31 provinces (Liu 2010), but it was not until 2013 that the Chinese government acknowledged their existence.

Meanwhile, water pollution affects more than half of China's rivers, lakes and urban groundwater. A 2014 Ministry of Land and Resources report found that 60 percent of groundwater was very poor or relatively poor, a deterioration from the year before. Twenty-eight percent of China's rivers were ranked at category worse than four on a Chinese scale of one to five, so toxic that they are unsuitable even for agricultural use. Some of China's major lakes, such as Dianchi in Yunnan, are ranked as severely polluted (Ministry of Environmental Protection 2014), despite the fact that billions have been invested to clean it up. A 2007 OECD study found that hundreds of millions of Chinese people drink water contaminated by arsenic, fluoride, untreated wastewater, fertilizers and pesticides. According to a State Oceanic Administration annual report, in 2014 some 38 out of 71 rivers enter the ocean with a water quality grade of "worse than Category V" – the grade unsuitable even for human touch. Eighty-one percent of China's coastal areas are severely contaminated, and half of the 445 monitored discharge points do not meet environmental standards. Not surprisingly, algae blooms are on the rise.

In addition to pollution problems, groundwater aquifers are rapidly being depleted as users dig deeper wells each year. Falling water tables in North China threaten the water supply of Beijing. The great Yellow River does not reliably flow all the way to the sea; in 1997, the worst year so far, it failed to reach the eastern delta for 226 days, essentially drying out. In a book originally published in Chinese in 1999, water pollution activist Ma Jun states that 400 out of 600 cities are facing water shortages, including 30 out of the 32 largest cities (2004). Attempting to deal with this threat, the Chinese government is building a three-channel "South–North Water Transfer Project" [*nanshui beidiao* 南水北调] to move water from the Yangzi to the Yellow River. This multi-billion-dollar megaproject comes with enormous negative environmental and social implications, including effects on irrigation in the South where farmers accustomed to access are being deprived of water, human rights implications for the forcibly relocated, problems with pollution in the channeled water, and devastating ecological impacts on the Tibetan Plateau should the Westernmost route be built (International Rivers Network n.d.).

Research studies have suggested that water stress could create massive numbers of dislocated "environmental refugees" in coming decades as large parts of China face water shortages (Shalizi 2006). The World Bank has estimated that more than 300 million people in rural China lack access to safe drinking water (Xie 2009). China's rainfall is already highly seasonal – with 70 percent falling during the rainy months and 30 percent during the dry – and geographically uneven. The North, with 60 percent of China's cropland, has only 16 percent of its water, while the South, with 40 percent of the cropland, has 84 percent (Loh 2011). When climate change, pollution, and overuse for irrigation and industry are added to this fundamentally insecure situation, the Chinese people's access to water becomes highly unpredictable.

Given the severity of these and other entrenched problems such as deforestation, erosion, desertification, soil contamination, heavy metal pollution, salinization, loss of arable land, acid rain, and biodiversity loss, China's handling of its environmental crisis has become of critical importance to the country's stability and the legitimacy of the government. The nation's environmental challenges are so severe and so central to the manner in which China will "rise" that it is no exaggeration to say that they cannot be separated from its national identity and the government's ability to provide for the Chinese people. Acute environmental degradation threatens social stability; increasingly, environmental protests trigger state concerns about broader unrest. "Environmental mass incidents" [*huanjing quntixing shijian* 环境群体性事件] sparked by local pollution are estimated to number 5,000 per year (Ma, Tianjie 2008/2009), with some reports putting the figure much higher. Numbers of environmental mass incidents in China have been increasing at an alarming annual rate of 29% since 1996. In a presentation to the National People's Congress, Yang Chaofei, a Ministry of Environmental Protection engineer, stated that in 2011, "major environmental incidents" had increased by 120% over the year before. Many of these involve only a small crowd or short protest and are resolved in a matter of hours, while others involve thousands of people and shut down major cities. In Kunming, the capital of Yunnan Province, May 2013 protests against a new refinery project led by one of China's oil giants caught national attention and only ended when the mayor of Kunming publicly committed that the project would not be approved without the agreement of the majority of citizens.

The Chinese Communist Party and the state government's controls of power are at stake as they try to achieve contradictory aims. They must provide an improvement in material living standards in a country whose hinterlands are still desperately poor and whose middle class is just beginning to discover the joys of consumption after decades of privation. At the same time, they must deal with industrial accidents, the environmental costs of the country's manufacturing so many of the world's consumer products, and growing resistance to toxic pollution. Despite being armed with some of the world's best environmental laws and regulations, China's bureaucracy faces huge challenges in implementation. Local incentives to cut corners on regulatory implementation and enforcement and to pursue polluting practices prevail. While some government officials and agencies are making serious attempts to shift the country to an alternative development model, these efforts often seem puny when pitted against powerful forces of corruption, decentralized authority structures beyond the reach of the law, and incentives to focus on economic growth to the exclusion of other considerations. China's civil society is still weak and mistrusted by central powers, so efforts to deal with severe environmental problems "from the bottom" through public pressure are also inadequate in the face of monumental problems. When one considers that there are also cultural factors that emphasize conspicuous consumption and mistrust of government authority, and even rationalize illegal behavior in the interest of financial gain, the challenges can seem very great indeed. As Jonathan Watts writes in *When a Billion Chinese Jump*, "China's political system now exhibits the worst elements of dictatorship and democracy: power lies neither at the top nor the bottom, but within a middle class of developers, polluters, and local officials who are difficult to regulate, monitor, and challenge" (2010b, p. 290).

China's environmental challenges are thus tied to domestic political structures, rapid economic growth, and an intense phase of globalization in which the entire planet is involved. We can productively use the lens of development studies to understand these dynamics, since China has so rapidly moved from being a less developed country to a transitional one to one that is already a superpower. The key question is whether this unprecedented development will be "sustainable."

The term sustainable development was articulated in 1987 in the United Nations World Commission on Environment and Development's report, *Our Common Future* (also known as the Brundtland Report) and is commonly defined as meeting the needs of present generations without endangering the ability of future generations to do the same (WCED 1987). In the Chinese context, the question can be phrased: Can Chinese people alive today pursue healthy and meaningful lives without stealing resources from their children or from vulnerable populations within the country and abroad? The sustainable development lens suggests other difficult ethical questions inherent in China's rise: Do the Chinese people have an inherent right to the higher living standards enjoyed in the developed world? To what extent are China's environmental problems due to the rest of the world's consumption patterns? Can Chinese cities improve their environments without shifting pollution to other, more vulnerable regions? Can China deal with the acute poverty in much of the country's Far West, even as eastern parts of the nation grow richer? What is the cultural and historical context in which China is trying to achieve sustainable development, and should it be embraced or rejected in the search for success? Finally, in a world of increasing limits on resources and pollution "sinks," or repositories, is it even possible to build an equitable world in which people enjoy equal access to resources without taking them from successive generations, from the vulnerable, or from other species? While these questions do not have definitive answers, they are well worth considering as members of the international community concerned about the planet's dire environmental situation seek to build alliances and craft solutions to collective challenges.

Five core analytical concepts can bring China's choices and prospects into relief: the implications of *globalization*, or the increasingly complex and powerful ties that bind China and the rest of the world; the challenges of *governance*, which expands the notion of what the government can and cannot do and of the reach of the state; contested *national identity*, where competing world views and value systems offer different interpretations of China's past, present, and future; the evolution of *civil society*, which helps us focus on the complex relationship between citizens' groups and power; and the problem of *environmental justice* and equity, which involves the displacement of environmental harm across time and space. These concepts are familiar to students and scholars of international relations, and each one will be explored more deeply in the chapters that follow. However, it will be helpful to introduce them briefly here so as to explain how they will be used in this volume.

GLOBALIZATION

For the purposes of this book, globalization can usefully be considered as a shrinkage of time and space due to the introduction and spread of technologies such as the Internet and air travel, and as an increase in the flow of goods, capital, people, and ideas across borders (Mittelman 2000). The interdependence of nations in the global economy continues to increase and grow more complex, while the pace of change in China's status and influence within that global trend is unprecedented. The flow of globalization extends in multiple directions, both outward and inward, like a complex web; China's economy has become so intertwined with the economies of the rest of the world that a shift in China's markets can be felt elsewhere almost immediately, and a shift elsewhere can be felt just as quickly in China.

For example, drought and loss of arable land to industry, which lead China to seek more grain on the world market, raises global food prices, pushing marginalized people elsewhere in the world toward desperation. China's monetary policies affect the balance of trade with the U.S. and other major powers, hence the volume and intensity of the flow of manufactured products. The U.S. debt crisis of 2011 infuriated Chinese investors, who questioned their government's willingness to purchase so many U.S. Treasury bonds, yet in effect China lends the U.S. government money to sustain its economy so that American consumers can purchase Chinese products. China's newfound ability to purchase real estate overseas and invest in multinational companies alters landscapes, both literally and figuratively. Massive foreign investment in China, both directly and through joint ventures, drives resource extraction and pollution, while China's foreign direct investment (FDI) does the same overseas. In sum, globalization, and China's interconnectedness with the world, explains many changes in China's environmental situation, both positive and negative.

The enormity of the change in China's status vis-à-vis the rest of the world may become clearer if we compare the late 1970s just after the death of Mao Zedong, when China was still largely isolated from the world, to today. A few of my personal recollections about the flow of goods, capital, people and ideas from the early days of the reforms may underscore the transformation China has experienced during these few short decades.

Goods

Immediately after the death of Mao in 1976, Chinese people were so afraid of being called capitalists that they hesitated to sell even a few vegetables. When the first few peasants began to gather at the gate of the college where I worked, offering a few bunches of spinach or a basket of eggs, the professors commented nervously on this dangerous "free market" [*ziyou shichang* 自由市场]. Both intellectuals and farmers had been severely criticized for capitalist leanings during the Cultural Revolution, some even "persecuted to death," as the Chinese phrase puts it, driven to severe ill-health or suicide. During the first few years of Communist Party Secretary Deng Xiaoping's post-Mao economic reforms, which allowed groups and even individuals to form profit-making enterprises and forced state-owned enterprises to be responsible for their own profits and losses, the government felt obliged to introduce a propaganda campaign to reassure the Chinese people that the days of being persecuted for accumulating wealth were over. The slogan went: "It's glorious to get rich" [*zhifu guangrong* 致富光荣]. Today, of course, China is the manufacturing hub of the world, as we discover easily when we look at the labels on our clothing, toys, and electronic equipment. When in March 2014 *Forbes* calculated the net worth of the world's billionaires, 152 on the list were from China, with only the U.S. claiming more, a 60% increase from two years before. Three Chinese energy companies held spots three, four, and seven in *Fortune* magazine's Global 500 list of the largest companies in 2014. Much of this industrial activity involved heavy pollution to produce goods for the global market. When an American family tried to live without Chinese-made goods, they found it so hard to do that they wrote a book about it (Bongiorni 2007).

Capital

The handful of Chinese who were able to visit the outside world during the late 1970s generally did so through organized exchange visits. They had little or no foreign currency to spend, for the *renminbi* (or *yuan*) was not freely convertible. In the early 1980s, on a short contract as a Mandarin interpreter for a group of government officials visiting the U.S., I was amused and somewhat saddened to see them collect ash-trays and soap from American hotel rooms, their only way of satisfying the enormous expectations of a gift-giving culture. Today, Chinese government investments have become so powerful that as of October 2014, the U.S. Treasury Department indicates, mainland China held 1.25 trillion dollars in U.S. public debt. This staggering sum illustrates the change in China's fortunes. The environmental implications of China's newfound buying power are enormous. To satisfy insecurities about supply of key resources, from grain to minerals to fossil fuels, the Chinese are buying land and influence, both in developed places like Vancouver and in the resource-rich developing world. Sometimes they do so through outright purchase, sometimes through investment. Another example of the power of Chinese capital is through foreign aid programs that persuaded holdout countries who recognized Taiwan as the legitimate government of China to change allegiances (among them Costa Rica, which received in thanks a fabulous 35,175-seat sports arena which opened in March 2011). Capital flows both ways:

FDI by multinational corporations, tied to global trade, is now a significant part of the Chinese economy; in 2014, reported foreign investment in China was $119.56 billion (Ministry of Commerce, P.R. China 2014).

People

The enormity of the change in the flow of people becomes clear when one considers that, immediately after Mao's death in 1976, the handful of foreigners who could get visas to visit China could reliably find each other changing planes in Tokyo's Narita airport or sitting in the lobby of the Beijing Hotel. Ordinary Chinese simply could not get a passport to travel abroad. My Hunan Teachers' College English-language students expected to spend their lives mastering and eventually teaching a language they would never use overseas and perhaps rarely employ to communicate with a native speaker. By the end of 2014, the Chinese Ministry of Education counted more than one-third of a million foreign students currently studying in China, while more than 3 million Chinese were studying overseas. Statistics from the Chinese Ministry of Human Resources and Labor Security showed 246,400 foreigners working in China in 2012, up slightly from the year before. Millions of Chinese now regularly travel abroad and the number is growing rapidly. In fiscal year 2013, according to U.S. Department of State figures, 32,825 Chinese born on the mainland were given immigrant visas, and more than 1.3 million non-immigrant visas were issued from the five U.S. consular posts in China. So attractive has the Chinese job market become for Westerners facing bleak employment prospects at home that some are even focusing their job searches there, despite growing concern about health impacts of pollution.

The flow of people facilitates the flow of ideas in both directions – the Chinese government is actively making it more attractive for

foreigners to study in China through English-language degree programs and PhD fellowships, part of a "soft power" strategy to spread its
influence through diplomacy and exchange. At the same time it is
finding it difficult to control the impact of foreign ideas, as was seen
quite dramatically and notoriously in Beijing during the U.N.'s 1995
Fourth World Conference on Women, where non-governmental
organizations (NGOs) were relegated to a location outside of Beijing
but nevertheless managed to express a vibrant level of civil society participation that left Chinese officials scrambling to try to exert control.
Cell phones and social networking technologies like *weibo*, the Chinese
equivalent of Twitter, WeChat, an influential social network platform
for sharing personal life, pictures, and news, and personal blogs have all
challenged state-run media. Numerous new mobile phone apps show
China ready to embrace the era of big data. One of the most popular,
the "China Air Quality Index," has thousands of downloads and has
become an essential tool for people to check real-time air quality and
decide what self-protection measures to take, such as keeping their
children indoors. The 2011 Arab Spring in Egypt and elsewhere in the
Middle East led the government to intensify efforts to control Internet
information and to censor references to a potential copycat "Jasmine
Revolution," using filters to cut communication in which the word
jasmine appeared (and causing headaches for buyers and sellers of tea
and perfume). Information about the 2014 "umbrella revolution"
of Hong Kong was tightly controlled out of concern that the pro-
democracy demonstrations could easily spread to the mainland.

Ideas

During the Mao years, the handful of approved foreign writers included
only the left-wing: Balzac, Tolstoy, Twain, London, and Dickens. I
vividly remember how people lined up for hours when the first

post-Cultural Revolution Western film, "The Sound of Music," was released for viewing in China. The Chinese had literally been cut off from the outside world; at the height of ultra-left extremism, even communicating with overseas relatives could mean death. After Mao died and the Four Modernizations (in agriculture, industry, defense, and science and technology) became national policy and were deemed to necessitate training in the English language, I became employed as the only foreign teacher at my university, the first since a Russian language teacher had been expelled in 1960 after the Sino-Soviet split. The responsibility for providing a bridge to so much missing information felt very great. Nowadays, the universities of Peking, Qinghua, Fudan and elsewhere rival the world's best, and foreign teachers and students are so numerous as to merit barely a glance. Even provincial universities, technical institutes, and high schools have English language classes and specific subject instructors from overseas.

While the flow of goods and capital provides much of the impetus for China's environmental problems, the flow of people and ideas also provides mitigating possibilities. Importantly for the subject of this book, environmental information flows relatively freely from the outside world, with blocked websites available to Chinese who know how to circumvent China's Internet firewalls. The Chinese effort to understand how to navigate their environmental crisis is reflected in increasing transparency of data about the impacts of pollution, climate change, and ozone depletion. Tactics and strategies of environmental non-governmental groups have evolved dramatically since the first environmental non-governmental organization (ENGO) was founded in 1994, as we shall see later in the book. Chinese government officials have long been major players in global environmental negotiations, and now Chinese citizens' groups are starting to participate as well. Foreign values like government and corporate accountability and the rule of law have also become goals for China, nurtured in part through extensive exchanges of legal professionals and intensive domestic debate among Chinese intellectuals and policy makers. Alternative energy technologies like solar, wind, and biomass have not only been widely adopted but are undergoing intense research and development, with heavy government investment and support; China has even become the world's leading exporter of solar panels, where manufacturers see tremendous opportunity for growth. Excitement over the creation of green jobs through a new green economy is growing (Pan et al. 2011). On the less positive side, Western-style consumption is portrayed and often distorted in films and other media, modeling lavish lifestyles and wasteful resource use that does not promote sustainability.

GOVERNANCE

The concept of governance, with its Latin root in "steering," broadens the study of politics beyond that of the state, with its laws, regulations, and "monopoly on the legitimate use of violence," as Max Weber so famously expressed it, to focus on the processes, policies, laws, and institutions that shape social relations and guide public attitudes and behavior. In the case of China, using this broader understanding helps us see the complexity and limitations of the government's efforts to implement environmental laws and regulations, to ensure a safer food supply, and to crack down on intellectual property violations. Environmentalists use the term "global governance" to draw attention to collective efforts to address transnational problems that states alone cannot solve, such as climate change, ozone depletion, overfishing, and threats to migratory and endangered species, especially given the international state system's relative absence of meaningfully enforceable or "hard" international environmental law. Non-governmental forces and actors such as citizens' groups participate in "steering" societies and shaping public behavior, often bypassing the state entirely. In thinking about governance, we may also find useful Michel Foucault's concept of "governmentality," which shifts attention from the state's power over death to its power over the ways that its citizens live. This is a useful concept for understanding authoritarian countries that seek to regulate important aspects of their citizens' lives, including customs and social structures affecting behavior and attitudes toward natural resources. For China this is particularly relevant in border areas, where traditional nomadic societies are being forced to "sedentarize," often in the name of environmental protection, and which often results in the destruction of their cultural identities and livelihoods.

NATIONAL IDENTITY

The Chinese people's struggles to define their national identity also provide us with important insights into China's environmental challenges. Every nation tells itself stories of where it has been and where it is going, thereby providing citizens with a shared understanding of the past and sense of the future. The stories are supported by myths, legends, and official renditions of national history; they are taught by families and schools and reinforced through national symbols such as the images on currency, flags, and statues. They are enacted and brought to life through rituals such as graduations, sporting events, school plays, religious ceremonies, and holiday traditions. The concept of national identity includes not only these stories but also people's value systems and world views. It captures ingrained cultural traits such as attitudes toward authority, the importance of the collective versus the individual, and understandings of what makes one people different from another. It captures perceptions of nature, the outdoors, and the relationship between people and animals. In the Chinese case, the concept also captures a competing self-understanding of the Chinese nation as both superior and inferior to others: China is both a great Middle Kingdom and a country recently humiliated by foreign imperialist powers, beginning with the great age of colonization. In this sense, China's rise is seen simply as a reclaiming of a rightful place in the world. The national sensitivity over rank and respect is undergirded and reinforced by a Confucian philosophy that sees harmonious societies as inherently hierarchical and emphasizes the importance of "face," or respect, in dealings with others. The correct performance of one's assigned social role within a network of personal connections is one of the highest cultural values, and demonstrating respect for one's superiors by "giving face" is a primary lubricant for good social and political relationships.

As this book will argue, the preoccupation with reasserting China's place of respect in the world underlies many of China's development decisions and helps us to understand the important role of national identity in China's prospects for achieving sustainable development. In its search for national greatness and improved living standards for more than a billion people, will China pursue the same level of wasteful consumption that Western powers have enjoyed and, if so, can the planet afford that? Or by "leapfrogging," using clean technologies, better forms of social organization focused on local communities, creating sustainable cities and clean transportation networks, and reviving agricultural systems that maintain the connection between farmer and consumer even in modern cities, is there a possibility that China can show the world a gentler, less destructive way of achieving high living standards and human development? Is there a possibility of reshaping national identity and the historical narrative in such a way that it promotes values of moderation, humility, and gentleness, or will "face" and conspicuous consumption continue to govern Chinese actions at home and abroad? These are core questions both for the Chinese people and for the planet. Some Chinese are plumbing their traditions for guidance, but for a Chinese style of environmentalism to gain broad acceptance, it will need to address national pride and the thirst for global leadership, power, and respect.

CIVIL SOCIETY

A concept closely related to governance is that of civil society, which can be understood as that space in society that exists between the level of the individual (or family, as some define it) and the state, where citizens come together "horizontally" and freely for shared purposes. Civil society can include advocacy groups such as Greenpeace or the International Fund for Animal Welfare, hobbyist clubs such as calligraphers and practitioners of tai chi (*taijiquan*), charitable organizations such as Wheelchair Foundation China, academic establishments such as universities and cram schools, religious institutions such as temples, mosques, and churches, as well as "illegal" groups such as Falungong and underground house churches. As the Italian political theorist Antonio Gramsci pointed out in his *Prison Notebooks*, written in the 1930s but still relevant for understanding contemporary societies, civil society is often "penetrated" by the state. The relationship is complex and often contested and ambivalent (Gramsci 1991). The state and its institutions use civil society groups to try to mould people into useful citizens, even as civil society groups attempt to influence and mould the state. Government-run schools teach approved curricula and reward certain behavior and types of learning through grades and examinations; families and religious institutions "socialize" us and teach us how to behave in ways that will allow us to succeed in the society into which we were born. In China, this relationship is particularly uneasy and the state works especially hard to control citizens' groups, including ENGOs, by requiring them to register and by monitoring their activities. At times the state refuses to recognize new groups, or even dissolves existing ones. However, the rising demands of the middle class for cleaner air and water, information transparency, and government accountability are important impetuses for a more articulate and powerful civil society, albeit one with "Chinese characteristics" of collaboration with friendly government forces.

ENVIRONMENTAL JUSTICE AND THE DISPLACEMENT OF ENVIRONMENTAL HARM

An important measurement used by those who study environmental politics is that of the environmental footprint. Individuals can take a simple online footprint quiz to calculate their impact on the planet. Schools and universities, corporations, towns, cities, and nations can use more sophisticated measures to calculate their sustainability index in order to create a baseline for improvement or to track changes in energy consumption, carbon usage, or other behavior they hope to improve. A footprint can even serve as a way of measuring a positive contribution, as when users of solar power send electricity back into the grid. Indeed, the concept of the carbon footprint underlies international negotiations on climate change, as each country agrees to strive toward a greenhouse gas emissions limit that it believes it can achieve without suffering devastating economic damage. Yet the calculation of the footprint of an individual, institution, or country often overlooks what Peter Dauvergne (1997) and others have called its "shadow ecology." From where does it extract the resources it consumes? To where does it export its waste? What are the hidden costs of daily consumption?

The final theme that will teach us about the underlying dynamics of China's environmental challenges is that of displacement of environmental harm, which is a close cousin to the concept of environmental justice. Powerful regions and states tend to displace destructive extractive activities and to shift toxic wastes to weaker or poorer communities, regions, and countries. They do so not necessarily out of malice; such dynamics are often cost-effective and driven by the market. Other factors such as investment incentives and access to raw materials also influence the movement of businesses around the world. Nonetheless, advocates for environmental justice have documented this relocation of harm as a common phenomenon at both transnational and domestic levels: Weak communities, regions, and states bear a disproportionate burden of the costs of economic activity, while wealthy ones enjoy most of the benefits. Immanuel Wallerstein (1979) has articulated a world systems theory describing a dynamic among "core, semi-periphery, and periphery" which may help explicate this process. Marginalized areas tend to enrich stronger ones through a process that shifts wealth. In the Chinese case, the "core" may generally be understood as the wealthy areas on the eastern coast, while the periphery is the poor western interior. We can also see this phenomenon at work within provinces. Industries gravitate to less developed areas within regions or outside the city limits, often with citizens and the government in developed areas pressing for industrial restructuring or clean-up, while local leaders in poor regions offer incentives in an effort to alleviate poverty and provide economic opportunities.

China's thirst for resources, from timber and wildlife to fossil fuels and minerals, has led to an increase in environmental degradation in places beyond its national boundaries, which has contributed to forests denuded of timber as far away as Liberia and to mountains gutted of coal as far away as Australia. At the same time, but less frequently noted in the Western media, consumers in developed countries have displaced many of the costs and benefits of manufacturing onto China and the Chinese people. By using the analytical lenses of environmental justice and displacement of environmental harm, we can more clearly understand that within China, as among states, there are winners and losers. We can try to avoid finger-pointing and appreciate more fully a core dynamic that underlies resource extraction and pollution throughout the world.

ACADEMIC DISCIPLINES AND THE STUDY OF ENVIRONMENTAL CHALLENGES

We conclude this introductory chapter with some reflections on how various academic disciplines approach environmental problems, as this may help readers to frame their own interests and articulate ideas for research projects. The most conventional way is by country study: The problems of Indonesia, South Africa, Myanmar, or of course China are the subject of numerous policy briefs, statistical analyses, planning documents, scholarly studies, and term papers. One could also conduct a comparative study of two or more countries by issue area – China as compared with India on sustainable energy policy, for example, or the U.S. as compared with the E.U. on climate change, or Costa Rica's protected areas as compared with those of China. Of course, this country-level approach is severely limited by the fact that environmental issues transcend political borders. Although national policy and response must be understood, environmental problems do not carry passports, and eco-regions rarely correspond to nation-states. Moreover, the country approach neglects inequality, regional variation, culture, and a host of other factors that may shape a state's environment.

Another important way of approaching environmental issues is to focus on sectors – water, energy, grasslands, wildlife, mining, agriculture, air – using a "resources" approach, which tends to emphasize the utility of these sectors for human beings. Or, we can become even more specific: We can focus on lakes, or on an individual lake such as Dianchi in Yunnan or Lake Tai in Eastern China, where clean-up efforts have been extensive, but to date have failed; or on rivers in general or on a specific river or watershed such as the Yangzi, Yellow, Pearl, Jinsha, or Nu. We can focus on a specific energy sector, such as China's achievements in the solar power market, or on nuclear power, focusing on China's ambitious plans to build many nuclear reactors. We can focus on hydropower dams, or on a specific dam such as the highly controversial Three Gorges Dam or the Zipingpu Dam, which narrowly missed collapse during the 2008 Sichuan earthquake and which some seismologists think might have contributed to the quake by shifting weight near a fault line. We can focus on a specific mineral such as coal, copper, zinc, or the "rare earths," which are used for defense, circuit boards, and solar panels, of which China produces more than 90 percent of global supplies. (China's withdrawal of rare earth export licenses for sale to Japan in 2010 was seen as a way to pressure its old rival over disputed islands in the East China Sea, and its control of the minerals has caused energy-efficient light bulb costs to skyrocket in the U.S.) We can focus on threats to a specific species, such as the beautiful and delicate Yangzi River dolphin which, sadly, is now gone forever, the only dolphin driven to extinction by human pollution and the noise of ships interfering with its communication abilities. Or we can study the plight of the giant panda, where conservation efforts reveal diverging philosophies, with some Chinese scientists focusing on captive breeding or even cloning, as compared to Western (and some Chinese) scientists emphasizing habitat conservation. We can focus on a specific event such as one of those listed in the next chapter – a specific oil spill, a specific earthquake, a specific accident or protest. We can organize our investigations according to key concepts, as we are doing in this book – globalization, governance, national identity, civil society, environmental justice. Or we can focus on an intransigent environmental problem such as the trade in wildlife and its relationship to traditional Chinese medicine, which understands food as a form of medicine and which considers all living creatures as potentially edible; or on illegal logging, using a commodity chain analysis which illuminates timber's dark journey; or on e-waste and its sources and impacts. Any of these issues could provide material for an entire book.

Let us also take a moment to consider the various scholarly disciplines and see what each might contribute in terms of interpretation and analysis. Scholars from all fields have become concerned about our planet's environmental crisis, and they have tried to use their theories, tools, and assumptions to consider the root causes of, and potential solutions to, environmental woes. In simplified form, here is a taste of how some of the disciplines might contribute to our understanding of China's environmental challenges.

Within the fields of political science and international relations, which tend to focus on the distribution and exertion of power, a range of schools of thought about global environmental politics is relevant for the study of Chinese environmental issues. "Neoliberal institutionalists" emphasize states' shared interests and study the organizations, treaties, declarations, and legal frameworks that contribute to the international governance of transboundary problem. They focus on bilateral, regional, and global cooperation on environmental issues and analyze how such institutions can be strengthened. For China, such scholars often analyze China's role in negotiations and participation in treaties and agreements. "Realists," however, often discredit these efforts to create global governance institutions, seeing them as ineffective. They understand the global state system as a zero-sum game, and tend toward a cynical view of the prospects that any of the great powers, including China, will curb their global quests for resources or create an equitable system for sharing them. By contrast, international relations "constructivists" focus on the importance of ideas and emphasize the role of scientific discoveries about climate change and ozone depletion, the political power of consensus groups like the Intergovernmental Panel on Climate Change or the International Union for the Conservation of Nature, and the evolving roles of global civil society and the media in creating pressure points for change. For them, how state power is projected is "socially constructed" and amenable to influence by issue framing, "naming and shaming," and other socialization techniques. Finally, "international political economists" focus on the role of global trade networks and regulations, the flow of goods and materials across borders, the direction of such flows (usually from developing countries to developed ones), and the movement of capital and role of corporations and multilateral development lending institutions like the World Bank. These varied approaches draw our attention to questions such as the nature of power in the modern world, the changeability of state interests, and the effectiveness of international institutional and legal arrangements. They also indicate different pathways into creating social change.

Other disciplines also have much to contribute to this conversation. Environmental anthropologists focus on the importance of culture, often through the subfield of religion and ecology. This lens is useful for looking at the intransigence of traditional beliefs such as the efficacy of medicine containing powdered tiger bones, for example, or at Confucianism's focus on the utility of nature as compared with Buddhism's reverence for life (and reincarnation) or Daoism's emphasis on adapting to nature or going with its flow. Political ecology, a subfield of geography or anthropology, focuses on how unequal power relationships among human beings affect land use and cause environmental degradation (Blaikie 1985). Similarly, sociologists, who often focus on the roles of race, class, and gender in social structure, have pioneered the subfields of environmental justice and social ecology, which argue that the human domination of nature is related to human domination of other humans (Bookchin 1980). For them, environmental degradation is essentially a product of inequality and injustice in the human world; we see their influence in concepts such as displacement of environmental harm and environmental racism. Meanwhile, environmental historians remind us that environmental degradation in China has been occurring for millennia, and they often use counterfactual reasoning to explain how events turned out as they did. Tigers might have survived in Southeast China, for example, if not for the deforestation which caused them to lose their habitat (Marks 2006). Environmental economists seek to measure the real costs of resource exploitation and degradation by assigning monetary value to goods formerly considered "free," such as publicly held forests and the atmosphere (considered part of the global commons). They try to create "green" accounting systems that measure "ecosystem services" such as water purification by wetlands and pollination by bees. In China, environmental economists have engaged in this effort and found it challenging because of the unreliability of Chinese statistics and the political sensitivity of the project. By contrast, ecological economists reject growth-oriented public policy as unsustainable and argue that we need to create a system that would create what Herman Daly (1996) has called a "steady state economy," or development without growth. This notion is related to the architect's notion of building a cradle-to-cradle economy rather than the cradle-to-grave system that currently drives economic transactions, such that all material goods can be reused indefinitely (McDonough and Braungart 2002).

These lenses on our subject produce fruitful insights, and we will be using a multidisciplinary approach in the pages ahead. Yet our chosen five core concepts will be most useful for organizing the subject at hand. Globalization, governance, national identity, civil society, and environmental justice derive primarily from political theory, anthropology, and political ecology, fields which I, the author, find to have compelling explanatory power. However, these concepts are far from exhaustive. Readers are encouraged to find their way more deeply into the issues raised in these pages through the approaches that most resonate for them, whether they are quantitative or qualitative, macro or micro, synchronic or diachronic, oriented toward international or national policy and law, or toward grassroots organizations or problems. Readers are also encouraged to read widely. Enjoyable first-person journalistic accounts can provide wonderful insight into Chinese environmental issues, particularly Jonathan Watts' well-researched and passionate *When a Billion Chinese Jump* (2010b). Also valuable are Colin Thubron's *Shadow of the Silk Road* (2007) and his earlier *Behind the Wall: A Journey through China* (1989). George Schaller's memoir, *The Last Panda* (1993), provides a wonderful account of WWF's encounters with the Chinese bureaucracy as the first Western environmental NGO in China. Peter Matthiessen's 1978 classic, *The Snow Leopard*, conveys the fragility, mystery, and beauty of the Tibetan Plateau, while Howard French's

2014 book on China's impact on Africa, *China's Second Continent*, uses compelling anecdotes to show how entrepreneurial Chinese are in effect colonizing the far corners of the globe. Similarly, Craig Simons' 2013 *Devouring Dragon* travels the world to understand China's global impact. Wonderful documentary films about China's environmental challenges such as "Warriors of Qiugang," "Beijing Besieged by Waste," and "Waking the Green Tiger" are now available; we mention some of the best of these at the ends of the chapters and hope you will use them to see both how polluted and how beautiful China can be, and to "meet" some of the public figures, activists, and ordinary people who play roles in this book. Recommended scholarly works can be found in the reference list.

OVERVIEW

The themes and analytical concepts of globalization, governance, national identity, civil society, and environmental justice will recur in the following chapters. The next chapter, which deepens our understanding of how globalization affects China's environmental challenges, presents broad trends, as well as drivers of China's environmental challenges such as population increase, the rise of the middle class, globalization and industrialization, urbanization and loss of arable land, and climate change. Chapter Three introduces the institutional and legal framework of China's governance system, which remains largely top-down even as limited decentralization has unleashed the market and empowered regional and local leaders. Chapter Four provides the historical and cultural context for China's changing national identity and the way decisions affecting sustainability are shaped by that context. Chapter Five investigates the changing possibilities for public participation in environmental governance, as well as civil society efforts to exert influence from the bottom up. Finally, Chapter Six investigates displacement of environmental harm across time and space, making the argument that China and the world are shifting the burden to future generations, to vulnerable populations in less powerful nations, within China proper to "peripheral" border areas primarily inhabited by ethnic minorities and the poor, to rural farmers, and to marginal urban populations. The final chapter argues that China and the planet are at a pivotal moment in which the choice for more sustainable development models is still available, but that making this choice will require humility, creativity, and rejection of business as usual. The window will not be open much longer. Failure to act in a timely fashion to slow the ongoing transformation of the planet may result in unspeakable harm to natural systems, biodiversity, and landscapes, and may destroy many of the ineffable qualities that make human life so precious, not only in China but elsewhere in the world. In this, the world's people have a common interest.

Like any author, I hope that this book will find a wide audience, not only in the West but also in China. I hope that this introduction to China's environmental challenges will spark debate, create appreciation for the complexity and difficulty of the choices that China faces, and promote the understanding that what happens on the other side of the world is ultimately also happening in one's own back yard. It does not pretend to be a complete account of the dynamics of environmental change in such a huge country; the pace of change is too rapid and local conditions are too varied. For this reason, every chapter ends not only with a list of questions for discussion but also with a list of additional resources, most of them accessible electronically. I hope that this book will empower readers to engage with these problems, to participate in the global effort to identify their solutions, and to understand that the decisions they make as citizens and consumers truly matter. The "butterfly effect" articulated by chaos theorist Edward Lorenz, which describes how a butterfly flapping its wings can eventually create a hurricane through a series of cascading events, is more relevant than ever in today's tightly interconnected world.

QUESTIONS FOR RESEARCH AND DISCUSSION

1 Do people in developing countries such as China have an inherent "right" to the same living standards as those in the developed world? If so, what mechanisms can help achieve such equity?

2 Can China develop first and clean up later, as much of the developed world did, or is this no longer an option? Can the international community reasonably expect the global South to follow a different path than that of the developed North? Does the developed world's standard of living have to change, or can new technologies and energy sources keep the planet from reaching ecological limits?

3 Can you apply the concepts of globalization, national identity, and environmental justice/displacement of harm to your country? How do they affect your country's environmental footprint?

4 Discuss the civil society groups of which you are a member or which are active in your community. Does the state play a role in these groups? Do these groups shape state or local policies? Do they shape your attitudes and behavior? How might the situation be different in China?

ADDITIONAL RESOURCES

- "China Dialogue." An online publication and blog about Chinese environmental issues in English and Chinese, available at www .chinadialogue.net.
- China Environment Forum, Woodrow Wilson International Center for Scholars in Washington, DC. Reports, publications, and lectures available online.

- Ecological footprint information and quizzes: http://www
.footprintnetwork.org and http://www.myfootprint.org
- Joseph Kahn and Jim Yardley, "Choking on Growth." Series and
discussion available on the *New York Times* website.

2 Environmental Challenges: _____
Drivers and Trends

The study of sustainability, whether long-term or short-term, local or global, inevitably engages questions of security, conflict, and threats to basic human welfare. Along with traditional security considerations such as military conflict over territory, scholars, policy makers, and development institutions are starting to understand threats to human well-being as coming from non-traditional sources. Environmental change may contribute to insecurity when people's livelihoods and basic needs are threatened. Environmental scarcity can create tension and dislocation, while "abundance" can also, ironically, create rivalry and spur conflict as powerful forces to try to gain control over valuable resources. Environmental change tends to initiate additional shifts in the form of feedback loops, as people respond to challenges with practices that often further degrade the land. Concepts like climate refugees, climate justice, and environmental security have become established in public discourse. As part of the effort to analyze and predict both international and domestic instability and to identify the conditions for a secure and meaningful human life, political institutions and development agencies have put great effort into identifying key trends and drivers of change. Major institutions that regularly issue relevant reports on China, and on Asia in general, include the World Bank, the Asian Development Bank, the U.N. Economic and Social Commission for Asia and the Pacific, and the Japan Environmental Council, as well as civil society groups with serious research agendas like Forest Trends and the World Resources Institute. Government institutions like the U.S. Department of State and the Congressional-Executive Commission on China also issue important annual reports that are well worth consulting.

For our purposes, salient current drivers of environmental change in China are similar to and yet different from the main drivers of change throughout the world. They include: population increase; the rise of the Chinese middle class and concomitant changes in their consumption patterns; globalization of trade and manufacturing, changes in land use and loss of arable land due to urbanization and development; and climate change, which induces glacier melt, sea-level rise, violent weather, droughts and floods, and ocean acidification. These underlying forces and trends that push transformation are often not immediately visible. They operate at a level that can seem removed from the events of day-to-day life. However, by identifying these drivers we can often project where societies are heading and understand more clearly why some problems are so very difficult to resolve. (Less quantifiable drivers of environmental change include the state itself, with government-driven development plans and policies, and China's complex historical legacy of nature conquest and political upheaval; these will be addressed elsewhere.) This chapter also provides an overview of key recent environmental events and incidents, beginning with the Songhua River benzene spill of 2005. It concludes with general trends in policy making, intellectual life, and public participation.

POPULATION INCREASE

Since the Communist Party took power in 1949, the Chinese population has more than doubled. A Mao-era saying, "Every mouth has two hands," helps explain why the government was slow to realize the negative implications of the exploding population for meeting development needs. Mao came to power as a soldier who appreciated the value of a large army, while China's Soviet "elder brother" the U.S.S.R., which dominated the post-1949 policy environment, had lost so many troops during World War II that it was rewarding women who had large families as "mother heroes." Ma Yinchu, the demographer who tried to warn Mao about the dangers of large families, was silenced during the 1957 Anti-rightist Movement. By the time the draconian one-child family policy was introduced in 1978, it was too late to stabilize the population at a size that would not strain China's resource base (Shapiro 2001). Nowadays, despite the sheer crush of the country's numbers, evident to anyone who has walked the streets of China's major cities, the government is more permissive about family size. This is because of the effectiveness of the last three decades' population control policies and growing concern about a shrinking workforce, in addition to a notable gender imbalance among newborns and an aging population with few dependants to care for its seniors. Rural couples whose first child is a girl, ethnic minorities, and people without siblings are generally permitted second children, and in December 2013 the government announced an additional relaxation policy that allows couples to have two children if either parent is an only child. In any event, China's enormous population size has made providing basic livelihoods for so many people, with such limited arable land, an enormous ongoing challenge.

For some Chinese analysts such as Qu Geping, the elder statesman of Chinese environmentalism and the author (with Li Jinchang) of a book called *Population and the Environment in China* (1994), almost all of China's environmental problems can be traced to overpopulation, including land availability, degradation of forests and grasslands, and scarcity of water, minerals, and energy. Qu takes a practical, if anthropocentric, view of conserving such "resources" as grasslands, forests, and minerals through improved population control, efficiency, and education. Qu, who attended the 1972 United Nations Conference on the Human Environment in Stockholm, was China's highest ranking environmental official for many years as Chairman of the Committee on

Environmental and Natural Resource Conservation in the National People's Congress. He also served as the top official in the State Environmental Protection Administration (now Ministry of Environmental Protection). The focus on the connection between overpopulation and environmental degradation is widespread among Chinese; if you ask about China's environmental problems, almost all mention what they call Mao's greatest mistake, his belief that "In many people strength is great" [ren duo liliang da 人多力量大].

The emphasis on human overpopulation as a root cause of environmental degradation is shared by many Western environmentalists, including Paul Ehrlich and John Holdren (1971), who are credited with creating an equation that describes environmental impact as a function of population, affluence, and technology (commonly written as the equation I = PAT). It seems obvious on the face of it that a growing human population exacerbates pressure on land and resources, increases pollution, and may actually surpass the "carrying capacity" of a geographic region or even the planet, leading to ecosystem vulnerability or collapse. Moreover, affluence obviously seems to bring greater consumption of goods, with all of the accompanying impacts on the earth. Technologies such as toxic chemicals and machines that allow us to extract resources are modern inventions which evidently contribute to the problem even as they seem to bring us higher standards of living and at times offer hope for environmental clean-up. That said, finding the root causes of environmental problems is not so easy, as problems tend to be interconnected via positive and negative feedback loops. The I = PAT equation leaves out so many key factors that some scholars have called it misleading or worse (Painter and Durham 1995). What is the root cause of overpopulation? Should we also be looking at government and family failure to educate little girls? Development professionals know that, statistically speaking, the better educated the woman, the smaller her family size. Should we look at social factors such as the lack of public assistance for retirees in the countryside, which make families feel as if they need many children, or at traditions of exogamy, in which the female joins her husband's family after marriage, leading to a preference for boys? Should we also look at the fact that in developing countries traditional families' power often rests on the size of their clan? Today, you will find many Chinese towns and villages that take their names from a single family, in an echo of the ongoing influence of that ancient political structure.

China's fertility rate is now low in global terms, and population is expected to peak in around 2025 at 1.4 billion; much of that population is aging, a fact of little consolation in a world set to reach a population of more than nine billion by 2050. Although urban Chinese were generally accepting of the one-child family policy and gender equality is well established in the cities, China's farmers, understandably worried about having enough hands to work the fields and sons to look after them in their old age, still favor boys. However, this may be changing. Increased urbanization in the countryside, or, as the Chinese slogan has it, "leave the land but don't leave the region" [litu bu lixiang 离土不离乡], may continue to lower birth rates overall, and so many rural Chinese are now migrating to large cities that conventional generalizations about rural versus urban birth rates may soon no longer apply.

RISE OF THE MIDDLE CLASS

Sheer numbers of people may not be as important as their consumption and production capabilities. Another key driver of environmental change and degradation is the global culture of affluence and consumption, a lifestyle and value system which has now been widely adopted in China. The growing middle class now aspires to own automobiles, live in spacious homes and apartments with comfortable and fashionable furnishings, eat higher up the food chain by switching from grain to meat-centered diets, and increase household energy use by using more appliances, heat, and air conditioning. Consumption patterns encourage resource extraction and production of luxury goods. For example, according to the Chinese Association of Automobile Manufacturers, the Chinese automobile market is the largest in the world with 25.1 million vehicles and an expansion of about 7 percent a year.

By some estimates, Chinese consumers purchase half of the world's luxury goods, including expensive brand-name products like watches, handbags, shoes, jewelry, alcohol, and clothes, this despite recent crackdowns on lavish spending and gift-giving among high government officials. The Chinese desire for the globalized Western lifestyle, modeled in films and observed through travel, is amplified by cultural traditions and recent history, which place a premium on conspicuous consumption, status symbols, and lavish gift-giving. The Chinese have suffered more than a century of privation and pent-up desire for material goods, and the newly affluent are enjoying their buying power to the utmost; Chinese international tourists are famously high spenders.

However, such consumption is fraught with risks and the low quality of Chinese products has become a shared global concern. All too often, "Made in China" means "Danger: Buyer Beware," as revealed during recent scandals over product quality of Chinese exports. Chinese cough syrup killed children in Panama while pesticide-contaminated Chinese spinach was banned in Japan. Fish can be full of antibiotics and heavy metals. Tire treads separate, drywall is tainted with asbestos, tainted pet food has caused renal failure in companion animals, toddlers' toys imported from China have been coated with lead paint, toothpaste sweetened with antifreeze. At home, Chinese consumers have lost confidence in the safety of their food, air, and water. This is reflected in the widespread purchase of bottled drinking water, which has itself often been drawn from the tap by unscrupulous sellers, and in the willingness to pay a premium for imported and "green" food products. In a reflection of consumer anxiety about food safety, by

2011, China had the fourth largest area of organic agricultural land in the world (Willer and Lernoud 2014). The importance of Chinese people's mistrust of their food sources cannot be overstated. In 2012, a survey carried out in 16 major Chinese cities asked urban residents to list "the most worrisome safety concerns." Food safety topped the list at 81.8 percent, with environmental safety at 20.1 percent. A 2012 investigation by one of China's leading magazines, *Caixin*, revealed that publicized food safety scandals represent only a fraction of unsafe food production practices, and a 2013 national survey conducted by the Chinese Academy of Social Sciences indicated that food safety (33.8%) and environmental quality (33.1%) held the two lowest rankings in public confidence level. In a return trip to Hunan in 2013, I witnessed my old professor friends' willingness to travel several hours to buy produce from a farmer they trusted, and their efforts to till a bit of soil outside their apartment building for themselves. I also saw many people climbing the Yuelu mountainside to line up and draw drinking water from a spring because of widespread fears of heavy metal contamination.

The newly affluent, in a better position to complain than the poor, are acutely aware of their dangerous and unhealthy living situations. Tainted food, unsafe consumer products, toxic air and water, and hazardous highways and public transportation systems mean that skyrocketing economic growth has done less to raise living standards than it appears. Citizen outrage is quick to ignite when a local accident or scandal occurs, creating a volatile and threatening situation for a government that struggles to hold onto its legitimacy and keep the populace disciplined.

Some environmentalists take heart in the rise of the middle class despite the increase in consumption and concomitant resource use. They cite the "environmental Kuznets curve," which posits a connection between income levels and environmental clean-up. According to this economic theory, which is popular among Chinese policy makers because it seems to justify taking more time to bring pollution under control, pollution tends to be high at early stages of national development, but when basic needs for material goods are met, citizens start to focus on less tangible quality-of-life issues such as clean air and water. They also acquire the political clout to demand them, resulting in an inverted U graph showing that a rising middle class correlates to an improvement in indicators of environmental degradation (Stern 2003). Examples of the middle class's impatience can be found in Beijing, where anger over polluted air spiked when the U.S. Embassy-Beijing began to release its rooftop air pollution monitoring data, and showed "hazardous" air on many days that the Chinese government's figures claimed its pollution was "moderate" or "slight" (Jacobs 2011); Chinese authorities were using an air quality standard missing the most hazardous fine particle "pm 2.5" (particulate matter smaller than 2.5 micrometers). A Chinese micro-blogger's poll on whether the government should adopt stricter standards elicited tens of thousands of votes in favor of immediate adoption, leading the Beijing air pollution monitoring center to start offering limited public tours and the country's environmental ministry to launch plans to monitor and disclose pm 2.5 particles in major Chinese cities.

Unfortunately, the Kuznets curve model when applied to the Chinese environment rests on shaky assumptions. It requires, first of all, that there be sufficient natural resources available to support and generate a middle class large enough to apply pressure to reduce pollution and environmental destruction. It also assumes that natural resources will be in a condition to be rehabilitated after development inflicts heavy damage. This is particularly questionable in the case of soil contamination and biodiversity loss. For the model to work, the government must be in a strong enough position to respond positively to middle class demands, which is far from the case in today's China, where good environmental laws and regulations often go ignored. In fact, despite the best efforts of some government regulators and policy makers, new industrial accidents and product and food safety scandals are in the news all the time. Finally, and most importantly, the planet cannot afford to wait for China to pass through the same stages of industrialization and clean-up followed in much of the developed world. The environmental Kuznets curve seems a pipe dream in the context of global patterns of environmental degradation. It indicates that the planet is at a tipping point with respect to many environmental indicators. Another model is required.

GLOBALIZATION OF MANUFACTURING

China's population numbers, and the people's growing affluence, may pale in significance as drivers of environmental change when one considers the globalized system of resource consumption and waste production to which they are connected. Much of the pollution that so troubles China's rising middle class is due to the fact that China has become a manufacturing powerhouse for the world. China's demand for resources is being driven not only by domestic consumers but also by international ones. We can more easily see the connection between China's problems and our own lifestyles if we consider the political economy of China's manufacture and export of consumer goods. The value of China's exports in 2013 made it number one in the world. As much as 94 percent of China's exports in recent years have been manufactured products such as electronics, toys, textiles, and furniture rather than agricultural products or fuels (WTO 2014) The huge scale of China's manufacturing apparatus is dramatically chronicled in the haunting documentary film "Manufactured Landscapes," which chronicles in slow-moving detail the football field-sized sweatshops powering China's economic growth and the world's consumption.

One of the most useful tools for understanding global political economy is "commodity chain analysis," which traces a given raw material from its source to the consumer. We can look at China's import of raw materials like minerals and timber from Southeast Asia and Africa and its export of finished products to developed countries, with 32 percent going to the European Union and United States alone (WTO 2014), although an increasing percentage of these products are destined for the Chinese domestic consumer. This analysis demonstrates that end-users in developed countries are key participants in a linked chain that moves from poor nations to rich ones, depleting "natural capital" that cannot be replenished.

Consider the example of wood products. As mentioned, in 1998 China suffered devastating floods prompting a government ban on logging on the headwaters of the Yangzi and other rivers in western China to protect watersheds from erosion and improve flood control. Although not always thoroughly enforced, the ban shifted logging, much of it illegal, to places such as Cambodia, Myanmar, Indonesia, Eastern Russia, and as far afield as Gabon. An investigation by the *Washington Post* followed the trail of illegal logging in Myanmar and other parts of Southeast Asia all the way to such Western retailers as Home Depot and IKEA. The dynamic works like this: Logs are harvested in countries with weak environmental laws and/or corrupt governments; officials are bribed (or actually conduct the business) at every step of the way and false papers are issued as the timber changes hands to disguise its illegal origins. It then crosses the border and brokers sell it to Chinese furniture factories that may or may not be aware of its origins. In this way, trees from the world's remaining tropical forests are converted into furniture, much of it exported to the West. In effect, China's growth depends on such imports of timber and other raw materials, so China's officials turn a blind eye. As the *Washington Post* put it, "The industry that connects forests in Asia with living rooms in the United States via the sawmills of China is a quintessential product of globalization" (Goodman and Finn 2007). According to researchers from the advocacy group Forest Trends, China's wood imports roughly tripled from 1997 (one year before the logging ban) to 2009. At the same time, the country's wood product exports have increased almost 700 percent in value (Sun and Canby 2010). When Western consumers make their purchases, few ask where the wood in their new patio set or designer flooring comes from, are aware of the Forest Stewardship Council's efforts to certify and promote sustainably harvested wood, or consider the tremendous rate at which the planet's last remaining tropical and old growth forests are being lost. Such commodity chain analysis can also be done for other reprocessed resources such as minerals, and it can be extended to uncover where such materials, including toxics, are discarded. It thus reveals the hidden costs of consumer buying power from a product's cradle to grave. Unfortunately, China's weak regulatory capacity is a problem for global "chain of custody" tracing efforts, since even well-meaning officials and factory managers have difficulty verifying the sources of their raw materials. Because China is in a dominant position in the middle of the commodity chain between loggers and consumers, without more active participation from China, efforts to create "sustainable" forest product certifications are doomed to fail.

LAND USE CHANGES: URBANIZATION, INDUSTRIALIZATION, AND LOSS OF FARMLAND

China is poorly endowed with farmable land and its water resources are unevenly distributed both geographically and seasonally. It has nearly a quarter of the world's population but only five percent of its water resources and seven percent of its arable land (Brandon 2011). China's limited farmland was squeezed to maximum productivity through centuries-old traditions of terracing, fertilizing, and irrigation, and fared especially poorly during the "war on nature" of the Mao years, which saw attacks on sparrows, rainforests, and wetlands as part of an effort to secure grain (Shapiro 2001). Pressure on the land has become more intense with rapid industrialization and real estate development.

Even the government acknowledges that some of the changes in Chinese land use are unsustainable, announcing a "red line" beyond which arable land should not be lost lest China's food security be at risk.

Like other Chinese statistics, figures on urbanization are unreliable, but some indicate that a billion Chinese people, or about 70 percent of the population, will live in cities by 2030. They will be concentrated in nearly 220 cities with populations of more than a million people, including eight megacities of more than 10 million inhabitants by 2025 (Woetzel et al. 2009). According to the National Bureau of Statistics of China, as of the end of 2011 for the first time more than half (51%) of all Chinese people were urban residents. New cities are being created in formerly rural areas to deal with unemployment and to try to stem migration to major cities, which the state views as a major challenge. Restrictions on residency rely upon the antiquated residence card system, which once kept farmers in place by limiting their holders' access to ration coupons for food and rights to obtain housing, education, and health care. Nowadays, with consumer goods so freely available on the open market, the residence card system has lost its power to restrain, and peasants often leave the countryside to join the "floating population" of temporary workers and housemaids in major urban centers. Numbers of these migrants had reached 245 million, or more than one-sixth of China's population, by the end of 2013. These are mostly rural farmers moving towards urban areas in pursuit of better-paid jobs and although they make up half of China's urban workforce, migrant workers remain the most socially marginalized group in China. Not only are they denied access to public services in the cities due to the household registration [*hukou* 户口] system, they are also subjected to exclusion and abuse (Pai 2012). Their children are not permitted to enroll in state schools, and informal schools that spring up are often abruptly dismantled as authorities seek to drive migrants back home. In addition to economic incentives, local officials are often keen to sell arable land to real estate developers as such sales are a prime source of income, creating a greater push toward urbanization. Farmers are often driven off the land against their will, without adequate compensation for loss of land and livelihood.

With arable land per capita only 40 percent of the world average (Zhou 2002), China's government strives to protect remaining farmland. In August 2011, *Xinhua* reported government desires to safeguard 1.8 billion *mu* (296 million acres) of arable land to shore up grain security. But the fast pace of urbanization and industrialization combined with other land use changes have threatened even that minimum area. According to a 2012 report by U.N. special rapporteur Olivier De Schutter,

> Since 1997, China has lost 8.2 million hectares (20.2 million acres) of arable land due to urbanization or industrialization, forest replanting programs, and damage caused by natural disasters ... This shrinking of arable land represents a major threat to the ability of China to maintain its current self-sufficiency in grain. An estimated 37 per cent of China's total territory suffers from land degradation. According to the Ministry of Land and Resources, about 12.3 million hectares – more than 10 per cent of the arable land in China – are contaminated by pollution. (UNOHCHR 2012)

More stringent central government farmland preservation policies have slowed the rate of loss, but local development speculators and government officials' land grabs for construction and development have become a source of widespread social conflict and unrest. In one of the most dramatic recent examples, in December 2011 thousands of residents of the fishing village of Wukan in Guangdong province revolted openly against the government for such seizures, a standoff that lasted more than a week and resulted in the death of at least one villager. Similar disputes, albeit smaller in scale, break out regularly, not least because so many farmers experience land appropriation, with compensation only a fraction of the value.

CLIMATE CHANGE

Climate change is both an outcome of environmental change and a major cause of it, and it is the last driver that we will consider here, although it may be the most devastating and difficult to control. Climate change alters rainfall patterns and promotes sea-level rise and strong storms, droughts and floods. These lead to cascading environmental effects such as desertification and erosion. Glacier melt in the Tibetan Plateau has an impact on the Yellow River and China's irrigation network in the North (Immerzeel et al. 2010). The aquifer below the huge alluvial North China Plain, fed by the increasingly parched Yellow River, is already falling by a meter per year and is set to be depleted within 25 years (Kahn and Yardley 2007). At the same time, aquifers that serve the huge city of Beijing continue to fall due to overuse for farming, industry, and household consumption. Extreme weather patterns have included violent storms and floods, while sustained droughts have been among the worst in centuries. Sea-level rise could challenge the spectacular modernization of coastal cities like Tianjin and Shanghai, where there are already plans to build a water gate to combat flooding from increased storms. International scholars published a detailed study suggesting that climate change could have devastated China's large Eastern cities (Balk et al. 2007), as the country's densely populated coastal areas are among the world's most vulnerable to sea-level rise and increased flooding from intense storms. Other organizations such as the Intergovernmental Panel on Climate Change have made similar forecasts for coastal areas throughout the world.

Chinese experts warn that climate change will also affect China's grain harvest, reducing yields of rice, wheat, and corn, threatening food security, and leading China to import more staple foods (which then has an impact on global prices). A November 9, 2011 *China Daily* article quoted Tang Huajun, a deputy dean of the Chinese Academy of Agricultural Sciences, as saying, "The impact of climate change, especially extreme weather and plant diseases and insects, will cause a bigger grain production fluctuation in China and bring more serious threats to the country's food supplies." This concern is underlined in the 2014 report of the Intergovernmental Panel on Climate Change, which warns strenuously of the negative impact of climate change on agricultural productivity and global food supplies.

Climate change directly degrades the environment, but it also exacerbates a feedback loop of human-induced secondary degradation when humans fail to adapt in an intelligent way: drought causes a need for increased irrigation, which all too often causes salinization and lowered water tables, causing further land stress, which then also leads to increased use of chemical fertilizers, which then leads to eutrophication, and so on. How China's government will approach the problem of "adaptation" (as distinct from "mitigation," which tries to address the causes rather than the effects), is a critical policy question for coming decades.

Almost all of China's major rivers flow from the glacier-rich Tibetan Plateau. When glaciers melt, rivers flood and then fail to replenish, and this threatens their basic ecological character and the life force that sustains China's population. China's per capita water resources are already among the lowest in the world, at just one-fourth of the world average (Xie 2009). There are mixed scientific findings as to the severity and timing of changes in glacier melt, and social, economic, and political as well as environmental drivers affect water scarcity in North China. As noted earlier, policy makers are so worried that North China, including Beijing, could run out of water that they have built channels to transfer water from the Yangzi to the Yellow River, a mega-project with its own problems of human rights abuses, forcible relocations of up to 300,000 people, and pollution (Freeman 2011). Yet if something is not done, massive water shortages could turn the people of North China into "climate refugees," people who are displaced because of environmental transformation due to climate change.

Another consequence of climate change is severe weather patterns. In Inner Mongolia and neighboring Ningxia province, sustained drought combined with severe winters has killed millions of cattle and forced farmers and herdsmen to dig ever-deeper wells. Nomads are being forced to settle in cities, with few urban skills. Meanwhile, in Central and Southern China, severe flooding after periods of drought has displaced entire towns and caused leaders to acknowledge their confidence in the massive Three Gorges Dam's capacity to control and withstand severe flooding may have been overly optimistic. Such natural disasters appear ever more common and severe, as is consistent with scientific predictions concerning the impacts of climate change.

China's own contribution to climate change is growing quickly. Chinese carbon emissions tripled between 1992 and 2007 (Minx et al. 2011). A definitive study from the University of East Anglia entitled "A Carbonizing Dragon" shows that China has overtaken the United States as the largest carbon emitter, primarily because of investment in heavy industry, infrastructure, and energy production. Ubanization is also a significant cause of increased emissions, as city living is more energy intensive than rural life. The Netherlands Environmental Assessment Agency has found that even on a per capita basis, Chinese emissions are on track to match or exceed those of the average American by 2017. Some believe this has already occurred.

As we shall see in more detail later in the book, the Chinese government is making strong efforts to deal with these problems. The "Scientific Development Perspective" [*kexue fazhan guan* 科学发展观], to use the official language of China's current guiding ideology, incorporates sustainable development and social welfare into the national goal of building a "Harmonious Society" [*hexie shehui* 和谐社会]. Chinese policy makers are well aware of the consequences of climate change, even as they argue that China is not responsible for most of it, and China is an eager recipient of "Clean Development Mechanism" funds and projects that reward developed countries for investing in climate change mitigating projects in the developing world (Morton 2005). China is reducing energy intensity per unit of GDP, establishing the largest carbon trading market in the world, and greatly increasing the percentage of renewables in its energy mix. A November 2014 U.S.–China agreement committed China to stop carbon emissions growth by 2030. But China's electricity and fuel challenges are great, and despite Chinese leadership in solar and wind manufacturing (it is the world's largest investor in these sectors), there is heavy reliance on domestic coal supplies and intense international competition to secure foreign supplies of fossil fuels. In 2013, coal made up 67.5 percent of China's energy use and oil made up 17.8 percent (BP Statistical Review of World Energy 2014). The good news is that, in conjunction with China's efforts to curb air pollution, top legislators recognize the urgency of addressing China's deep-rooted coal dependency. The "ten tough measures" released by the State Council in September 2013 have for the first time set caps on the nation's ever-increasing coal consumption. Achieving this ambitious plan, however, remains challenging given the uneven economic and social landscapes and the often unaligned targets among provincial and local governments. China is thus expected to continue to emit huge quantities of carbon dioxide. Its energy policy is expected to continue to emphasize energy intensity and increasing percentages of renewables (which China defines as including the often controversial big hydropower dams and nuclear power plants), while the use of fossil fuels in absolute numbers continues to rise.

Such trends are not inevitable. A November 2011 conference of the China Council of International Cooperation on Environment and Development, a group of 200 world experts on environmental policy who offer suggestions to the Chinese government, recommended that the country spend 5.77 trillion *yuan*, or about 909 billion dollars, before 2015 to make transitions away from polluting and energy-intensive industries. This would cost the country almost a million jobs and more than 100 billion *yuan* in economic output but save 1.43 trillion *yuan* in energy expenses while creating more than 10 million jobs and expanding the economy by more than 8 trillion *yuan*. The report warned that "the blind pursuit of economic growth has now become a huge obstacle for China's green growth," and that even with such investments, by 2020 the country will still face grave air pollution, water shortages, ecological degradation, and mounting piles of hazardous wastes (Li, Jing 2011).

RECENT EVENTS AND ENVIRONMENTAL CONFLICTS

Such drivers of environmental change as population growth, the rise of the middle class, globalization of manufacturing, land use changes, and climate change are difficult for the average person to perceive because they tend to be gradual and their impacts indirect. If you were to ask a Chinese citizen about the environment, he or she would probably mention instead the pernicious pollution levels that foul the air and water, recent industrial accidents, food safety scandals, disputes over polluting factories, and contention over infrastructure projects. He or she might also focus on regional problems, such as the overuse, pollution, and salinization of the Pearl River, which threaten the water supply of Guangzhou and Macao, or on local problems such as the solid waste crisis occurring in Beijing and elsewhere. A Chinese citizen might also mention specific endangered species that have been widely discussed in the media in recent years, including pandas, the Tibetan antelope, Yunnan golden monkeys, or the Yangzi River dolphin.

Here are just a few of the most well-known events of recent years, all of which would be familiar to any educated Chinese person concerned about environmental problems, and at least some of which may reflect the deep drivers of change listed above.

In November 2005, an explosion at a government-owned petrochemical plant in Jilin City caused a major spill of benzene, a highly carcinogenic chemical, into the Songhua River. This failure to maintain industrial production safety standards became an international incident. The government, whether out of insecurity or fear, failed to disclose the accident in a timely fashion either to the citizens of downriver Harbin city, whose water supply was eventually shut off, or to the government of downstream Russia and the affected citizens living along the Heilong River in the neighboring Russian Far East. ("Duty to Notify" is considered a principle of customary international environmental law.)

In April 2007, water quality "eco-warrior" Wu Lihong, a crusader against industrial pollution in Jiangsu Province's Lake Tai was arrested as a troublemaker for giving interviews to foreign journalists. He was officially charged with blackmailing the factories he was trying to shut down. His repression underlines the political risks that environmentalists and activist lawyers often face in an age of intense industrialization and globalization. In May 2007, a blue-green algae outbreak in the lake caused a drinking water crisis in the city of Wuxi on Lake Tai, causing bottled water prices to rise to six times their normal price.

Also in May 2007, cell phone text message-organized citizen resistance to a proposed Taiwan-China joint venture paraxylene (PX) chemical plant in Xiamen succeeded after a public demonstration of more than 20,000 residents gained the attention of local Party officials and the National People's Congress. One million text messages were sent warning that the chemical would cause birth deformities and leukemia. The factory was moved to a less well-organized community in Zhangzhou, illustrating the fact that middle-class resistance to pollution does not in itself result in environmental improvements.

In May 2008, a devastating earthquake in Sichuan Province's Wenchuan County killed about 70,000 people, many of them children whose schools collapsed due to shoddy construction. Some environmentalists and geologists believe that the weight of the water in the reservoir behind the Zipingpu dam on the Min River, located only a few kilometers from a major fault line, may have contributed to seismic instability in the region or even triggered the quake.

The 2008 Olympics, held just a few months afterwards in August, marked the culmination of a period of intense attention to air pollution in Beijing. There was so much doubt about air quality that some athletes remained in Japan until the last possible moment and emerged from airplanes wearing face masks, to the chagrin of Chinese hosts. The Chinese government exerted extraordinary efforts to ensure a blue skies event, building new subway lines, closing factories, and banning cars. They even seeded the clouds to induce rainfall in the days before the event to help settle pollution and ensure good weather for the opening ceremonies. Patriotic Chinese saw the successful event as a coming-out party for their country's re-entry to high status on the world stage, but pollution levels quickly returned to prior high levels after the Olympics ended. Urban air quality improved briefly when factories like the notorious Capital Iron and Steel Factory Company were moved to rural areas; however, high levels of pollutants still plague Beijing. This is driven in part by a massive increase in automobile sales and traffic. In January 2013, the "crazy bad" air pollution was so high as to be unmeasurable; flights were canceled and residents were told to stay indoors.

Also in 2008, there was increased global attention to e-waste villages in Guangdong Province, where many cast-offs of global trade in electronic equipment are recycled. A 2008 report broadcast in the U.S. on CBS television's "60 Minutes" spurred China to pass new regulations on recycling electronic equipment and to try to crack down on the lucrative illegal trade, but loopholes and problems with enforcement continue.

The years 2008 and 2009 saw protests and violent crackdowns in ethnic minority regions. In Lhasa, Tibet, a March 2008 protest soon spread to Tibetan areas in Sichuan, Qinghai, and Gansu Provinces. In July 2009 a violent riot occurred in the capital city of Urumqi in the Xinjiang Autonomous Region; incidents reflecting Muslim–Han tensions are ongoing and have even spread to other parts of China. There is a long history of Tibetan and Muslim resentment of Han Chinese rule, but recent tensions have been exacerbated for multiple reasons, including infrastructure projects that facilitate the state's resource extraction; Han in-migration; and social policies that promote tighter social control over nomads and dissenters. Nomads are made scapegoats for grasslands degradation that has much to do with policies that opened up remote territories, drained wetlands, and increased livestock during the Mao era.

In July 2010, two oil pipelines offloading imported crude oil from a tanker to a storage facility in China's Northeast port city of Dalian exploded, causing China's worst ever oil spill. A heroic clean-up by citizen volunteers and the People's Liberation Army masked uncertainty about the causes and size of the enormous spill.

In April–June 2011, 5,000 metric tons of chromium-contaminated carcinogenic chemicals were dumped in Yunnan Province's Qiujing Prefecture near the Chachong reservoir, threatening the Pearl River, which is the source of drinking water for tens of millions of people, including Guangzhou (Canton). In August, after 77 cattle died, police detained the two drivers and other employees of the trucking company that had been contracted to carry the waste to Guizhou Province.

The same year, the word "PX" was again back in news headlines when panic arose from a possible leak in a damaged storage tank in Dalian as a result of a typhoon. Tens of thousands of locals took to the streets. In response, the local government had to stop production and announce a relocation plan. Since then, PX projects have been increasingly demonized.

In January 2012 a mining company's illegal cadmium discharges contaminated two rivers in Guangxi province, killing fish and contaminating water supplies for 3.7 million people.

In March 2013, 16,000 dead pigs were discovered in a tributary of the Huangpu River, which supplies tap water to Shanghai. Tests showed they were infected with porcine circovirus and had presumably been dumped in the river.

In November the same year, a major explosion of a leaking oil pipeline in a residential area of Qingdao city caused 62 deaths and an oil spill of 3,000 square meters in beautiful Jiaozhou Bay. Residents criticized the local government and Sinopec, the responsible oil company, for their failure to organize effective emergency evacuation and for their delay in notifying the public of the leak when it was detected seven hours before the explosion.

In Beijing, recent years have seen multiple crippling smog events. "Airpocalypse" incidents associated with coal-burning and stagnant weather patterns have caused Beijing residents to turn to crisis mode. In November 2014, in an effort to clear the sky and provide an "APEC Blue" experience for visiting world leaders, the government adopted extreme measures such as forbidding the burning of funeral paper money, shutting down industry and many government offices, and banning cars. Ordinary people were enraged that foreigners were treated as more important than them, and correctly predicted the return of "revenge smog" as industries started up again.

In August 2015, chemical explosions in a hazardous materials warehouse in the major port city of Tianjin created a huge fireball of toxic gas, including the deadly sodium cyanide, killing more than 100. Government censorship of the internet and media sparked widespread protests.

The above list of recent environment-connected incidents could run to many more pages, including well-known localized struggles over the locations of waste incineration plants and publicity over "cancer villages," as well as ongoing campaigns against dam-building on rivers in Western China, most famously on the Nu River in Yunnan Province, where local leaders find the temptation to harness one of China's last remaining wild rivers for energy all but irresistible. We will explore some of these struggles in more detail in later chapters.

These newsworthy incidents and events have been accompanied by tremendous intellectual ferment and discussion at top policy-making levels, in think tanks and environmental NGOs, on university campuses, and among interested and affected ordinary citizens. Such open debate would have been all but impossible even a few decades ago. The educated public is paying increased attention to the connection between pollution and public health. Prominent groups such as Greenpeace and former journalist Ma Jun's Institute of Public and Environmental Affairs are creating pressure for greater information transparency on water and air pollution. From the central government's perspective, public anger over inequality, corruption, and pollution is so intense that it is understood as a threat to the regime. It is thus trying to institutionalize ways to reward local officials for environmental protection rather than economic growth, albeit with uneven success. Scholars, policy makers and activists are creating cutting-edge initiatives to try to shift China toward a sustainable development model, particularly through innovations in energy technology and pricing. Climate change is gaining greater public attention, as the droughts in Northern China have an impact on food prices and are being explicitly linked to extreme weather and Himalayan glacier melt. Moreover, as elsewhere in the world, the Chinese are starting to focus on the effects of climate change on parks and protected areas, whose fixed boundaries cannot easily shift to reflect ecosystem changes.

As we have seen in this overview of trends and drivers as well as specific recent events, China is undergoing radical economic, social, and environmental change, perhaps unprecedented in world history: To be Chinese today is to face incredible opportunities and challenges. The factors outlined above express themselves in China in particular ways, and how China responds to them rests on specific governance structures that have evolved over the course of China's unique history, as we shall see in the coming pages.

QUESTIONS FOR RESEARCH AND DISCUSSION

1 Identify an environmental problem in your country or in China and draw a flowchart that captures its root causes and consequences. How might scholars from different disciplines approach the problem? Which perspectives do you find most useful? Which are most likely to point to solutions?

2 Examine the products in your home and note where they were manufactured. How many come from China? Do you know where the raw materials in these products come from?

3 View Annie Leonard's 20-minute video, "Story of Stuff" (http://www.storyofstuff.org/movies-all/story-of-stuff/). Do you agree with the depiction of consumption in the global political economy? What is China's role? What is your personal role?

4 How is climate change affecting the place where you live? How noticeable are the direct or indirect effects? How are citizens and the government responding?

ADDITIONAL RESOURCES

- Asian Development Bank, China reports, available at: http://beta.adb.org/countries/prc/main
- Peter S. Goodman and Peter Finn, "Corruption Stains Timber Trade," *Washington Post*, Sunday April 1, 2007. Article available on the *Washington Post* website.

- "Manufactured Landscapes," a documentary by Jennifer Baichwal about photographer Edward Burtynsky. Excerpts available on YouTube.
- McKinsey Global Institute interactive website on China's urbanization and other trends: http://www.mckinsey.com/Insights/MGI/Research/Urbanization/Preparing_for_urban_billion_in_China
- South-North Water Diversion Project Commission of the State Council (English): http://www.nsbd.gov.cn/zx/english
- United Nations Economic and Social Commission for Asia and the Pacific: http://www.unescap.org
- World Bank development indicators and China reports, available at http://data.worldbank.org/country/china

3 | State-led Environmentalism: _____
The View from Above

China remains a top-down, centralized, authoritarian state. This is true even despite the enormous new personal and economic freedoms of the past quarter-century and the emergence of a vital middle class coming into their own both as consumers acquiring material goods and as citizens demanding government accountability. Civil initiatives remain sharply curtailed, NGO activities are circumscribed, and the administrative and legal systems that might help China to enforce its many excellent environmental laws remain weak. Well-intentioned environmental initiatives are often implemented in heavy-handed fashion, with negative implications for social justice. For example, Chinese citizens are being forcibly relocated in the name of such projects as the South-North Water Transfer Project, which is intended to carry water from the flood-prone Yangzi to the parched Yellow River from which North China gets its drinking water; minorities are subjected to "ecological migration," resettled into towns and cities from the grasslands of Inner Mongolia, Qinghai, Gansu and other parts of Greater Tibet in an effort to reduce the impact of herding; and the Three Gorges Dam alone has caused at least 1.2 million people to leave their homes, sometimes against their will and without the subsidies they have been promised, with more relocations to come because of unexpected problems with erosion. Millions more people across China are slated to be moved for initiatives to provide water, energy, and ecosystem restoration. Restrictions on public participation, debate, and access to information have meant the science used to develop policies for sustainable development does not always reflect local conditions or human impacts, and even contributes to official abuses of power. Indeed, China exhibits all the elements described in James Scott's 1998 classic, *Seeing Like a State*, which describes how well-intentioned "schemes to improve the human condition" often result in failure when a state is authoritarian, wedded to modernist ideology, and willing to relocate populations in order to make them "legible," especially under conditions when civil society is weak.

Nevertheless, the Chinese central government deserves tremendous credit for trying to integrate environmental concerns into its plans, laws, and policies. One of the most significant trends in the past few decades is the growing importance of sustainable development in national planning documents and central-level statements and commitments. The Chinese state has moved away from its Mao-era isolation and public self-presentation as a developing country that needs the world's assistance and is becoming a constructive participant in the global dialogue on how to resolve major transnational challenges. Environmental issues have climbed toward the top of the domestic agenda of China's leading officials. This is in response to growing public clamor about the impacts of pollution on health and quality of life, along with anger at corruption and growing social inequality. Policy makers at the highest levels of government have affirmed China's commitments to deal with the country's responsibility to mitigate global climate change, to improve energy efficiency, to carry out wide-scale conservation projects and stem desertification, and to tackle the intransigent problems of water and air pollution. Although there is an enormous implementation gap, these expressions of intention and commitment from the highest leadership are remarkable. In a typically outspoken and widely quoted comment, Deputy Environment Minister Pan Yue said in 2004, "If we continue on this path of traditional industrial civilization, there is no chance that we will have sustainable development. China's population, resources, environment have already reached the limits of their capacity to cope. Sustainable development and new sources of energy are the only roads we can take."

This chapter outlines what the Chinese government has done to shift toward sustainable development. It discusses how that narrative fits into the Chinese desire to regain stature on the international stage by participating in negotiations and treaties and perhaps by pioneering a new development model that "leapfrogs" some of the mistakes of Western countries (Pan et al. 2011). While the desire to regain national greatness might seem to compete with the effort to achieve sustainable development, there is another, perhaps more encouraging way of looking at the Chinese government's choices: China can follow the Western version of industrial modernization, which has often involved unjust, ecologically destructive economic development, or the country can create a post-industrial idea of progress that embraces the tenets of sustainability. This debate is complex and involves a range of individuals, bureaucratic institutions, and locations.

GOVERNMENT STRUCTURE

There is fragmentation, both horizontal and vertical, in China's governmental structure. Competing and overlapping bureaucracies plague every level of administration, and the lines of authority from the "center" in Beijing to the localities are often weak, with environmental officials at the prefecture, district, county, and township levels often answering to other local officials rather than to their superiors in the central environmental bureaucracy. As a result there are competing perspectives on development and environment within the state, and differences of opinion as to how much attention to pay to the environment. Within the bureaucratic system there are strong advocates for a new, more ecological form of modernization, but they face serious challenges. The desire for sustainability competes with a "pollute first, mitigate later" [*xianwuran houzhili* 先污染后治理] ethos found in many branches of the government as well as among regional and local leaders. These officials claim they are merely following the same pattern of development as modern industrialized nations and are too poor to prioritize environmental considerations.

To stimulate economic development and address poverty and potential unrest, China's leaders have in recent decades embarked on a program of decentralization, ceding many political and economic functions to the provincial and local levels. This has liberated economic actors, unleashing economic growth and entrepreneurial energy. However, such moves have made environmental policy implementation more difficult. The Ministry of Environmental Protection is attempting to exert strong centralized policy making and improve its weak implementation capacity at a time when local provinces, cities, and even towns enjoy great economic and political autonomy. As a Chinese saying goes, "the heavens are high and the emperor is far away" [*tiangao huangdiyuan* 天高皇帝远].

In private conversations and even in official documents and news articles, central-level environmental officials often reveal frustration with provincial and local cadres. They complain that as soon as their backs are turned, local officials return to their polluting ways, reopening dangerous illegal coal mines or resuming timber-cutting despite the logging ban. In 2006, the *South China Morning Post* quoted a top environmental official as blaming "the blind pursuit of economic development among local cadres over environmental protection" for problems with as many as half of the 21,000 chemical plants on the Yellow and Yangzi rivers, many of which expel effluent and were built without undergoing environmental impact assessments. Entrenched and corrupt power elites in remote areas sometimes act as if they hold sway over private fiefdoms, as confirmed through my own observations during a 2009 visit to Songpan, a town in Sichuan Province where local officials had appropriated for their own purposes a jeep purchased by a European ENGO. A pair of local Chinese women I befriended on a hike in the hills told me that the same clan had controlled the town since the Cultural Revolution, and that wounds from that period remained raw.

Understanding the institutional, legal, and bureaucratic framework in which China's environmental policy making and implementation take place requires an introduction to the structure of the Ministry of Environmental Protection (MEP), regional and local Environmental Protection Bureaus (EPBs) and Offices, and environmental legal framework. It also requires an overview of China's participation in international treaties and meetings in greater detail than that provided in prior chapters and a deeper appreciation of the challenges of implementation and enforcement.

The Communist Party of China is the unitary governing party, despite the nominal existence of a "united front" of other parties. The General Secretary is the most important national leader (Xi Jinping – who succeeded Hu Jintao in November 2012). There is a Politburo of 24 members, among which the Standing Committee, usually 9 members, is most powerful. Trying to penetrate the opaque process of coalition building and jockeying by which leaders emerge is a major preoccupation of foreign China-watchers. Alongside the Party, and still largely controlled by it, are State government institutions, with the nearly 3,000-member National People's Congress (NPC) approving laws and the general direction of the country through five-year plans negotiated in advance of their meetings. Although the NPC has traditionally been a rubber-stamping body for the Party, it has in recent years shown more independence, as in 1992 when about one-third of the members refused to approve the Three Gorges Dam. The NPC elects a Premier, currently Li Keqiang, who was originally trained as an economist, and approves a Work Report that often indicates the country's policy priorities.

The State Council of the People's Republic of China is the chief administrative authority in the country, chaired by the Premier. Several of the 25 ministries and commissions under the State Council have overlapping jurisdiction over environmental matters, including the Ministry of Environmental Protection (MEP), Ministry of Water Resources, Ministry of Agriculture, Ministry of Housing and Urban-Rural Development (formerly Ministry of Construction), Ministry of Science and Technology, Ministry of Land and Resources, and National Development and Reform Commission (NDRC), which oversees China's energy policy, including emissions reductions. At an administrative rank below the ministry level sits the State Forestry Administration. As an example of jurisdictional overlap, the MEP, Ministry of Land and Resources, Ministry of Housing and Urban-Rural Development, and State Forestry Administration have jurisdiction over aspects of the establishment and administration of national and provincial parks. In addition to the MEP, the Ministry of Foreign Affairs has responsibility for negotiating China's international role in environmental treaties and obligations in accordance with positions decided by the Party.

POLICY AND LAW

China has signed or ratified many international environmental treaties. These include: the 1971 Ramsar Convention on Wetlands, the 1973 Convention on International Trade in Endangered Species (CITES), the 1987 Montreal Protocol on Substances That Deplete the Ozone Layer, the 1989 Basel Convention on the Control of Transboundary Movements of Hazardous Wastes and their Disposal, the 1992 United Nations Framework Convention on Climate Change (UNFCCC), the 1997 Kyoto Protocol to the UNFCCC, and the most recent global environmental treaty, the 2013 Minamata Convention on Mercury. Chinese officials have attended the key U.N. conferences, including the pivotal global environmental conferences in 1972 in Stockholm, 1992 in Rio, 2002 in Johannesburg, and 2012 again in Rio. As a member of the negotiating bloc known as "China and the G-77," China has often helped to articulate developing countries' objections to being asked to pay the price of developed countries' industrial revolutions and high rates of consumption. Since 1994, it has also had an administrative center for China's Agenda 21, the sustainable development action plan to reduce poverty and conserve and manage resources that emerged during the Earth Summit at Rio in 1992. Despite the fact that Agenda 21 is generally understood to be a weak institution, China gives it more attention than many developed countries. Moreover, the country has done a great deal to reduce the percentage of non-renewable fossil fuel resources in its energy mix. This is remarkable since China had a reputation for many years as being a spoiler in climate change negotiations. Government negotiators often insisted that as a developing country China had no obligation to undertake firm commitments to reduce its carbon dioxide emissions; it was not responsible for creating the crisis and had an unshakable right to development. Nevertheless, in the 2011–15 12th Five-Year Plan, dubbed the greenest in China's history, China committed to further reduce its energy intensity by 16 percent, having already reduced it by 20 percent during the 11th Five-Year Plan. (Energy intensity measures an entity or country's efficiency of energy use per unit of GDP, as compared with absolute consumption.) It also pledged to shift its energy mix to 11.4 percent renewables (Lam 2011). China's five-year plans are designed to be roadmaps for top policy goals. They can be understood as key indicators of the directions and changes in development philosophy at the highest levels of Chinese leadership, making these figures highly significant. The 13th Five-Year Plan is expected to set even more aggressive targets. If everything goes as planned China's carbon emissions will have peaked by 2030, a remarkable achievement by any standards, albeit insufficient to halt the earth's progression to catastrophic warming. It appears that, in practice, China has accepted the principle of "common but differentiated responsibilities," a core tenet of international environmental law acknowledging that all countries have a shared interest in dealing with our environmental crises.

The overall positive environmental impact of these efforts may be less than it appears, as the "renewable" mix includes hydropower and nuclear plants, which come with their own, often severe, environmental and social problems. Ecosystem disruption, forcible relocations, illegal approval processes and shoddy construction plague China's dams. Furthermore, battles over dams on the remaining free-flowing rivers in China are being fought in villages and in the courts, with opponents alleging inadequate environmental impact assessments, poor compensation plans for displaced people, and corruption by local officials who stand to benefit from dam construction. There is a vigorous and articulate anti-dam opposition movement, both within China and in alliance with international groups. These are helping to focus attention on the dams China is building on the headwaters of international rivers, which may have significant negative impact on peaceful relations with neighboring states (Chellaney 2013). Nuclear energy has short-term and long-term risks of radiation leaks, meltdowns and other disasters, in addition to immediate impacts on aquatic life near cooling systems. Considering China's terrible safety record in other industrial projects such as coal mines and factories, China would do well to tread carefully. According to the World Nuclear Association, China had 24 nuclear power plants and 25 more under construction as of 2015, with the intention of tripling capacity in the near future and dramatically increasing it by 2050. Although approvals for new plants were briefly frozen after the March 2011 nuclear accident at the Japanese Fukushima plant, the new climate commitments suggest that nuclear power will be a major part of the equation. However, the renewable energy picture has bright spots: There have also been impressive strides in the production of wind energy, particularly in Inner Mongolia (which has yet to be well integrated into the energy grid). Solar energy also holds great promise, particularly in sun-drenched Tibet, where small-scale solar technology is widely adopted for greenhouses and cooking, and larger solar plants are used in enterprises and industry. This protects vegetation while bringing energy into homes far from the conventional grid.

In a striking shift toward conservation, the number of national parks in China has steadily increased to more than 200, most of them falling under the jurisdiction of the Ministry of Housing and Urban-Rural Construction. Although a great many of these are "paper parks" that exist in official documents and regulations but not in practice, China is beginning to experiment with new management styles, in some cases charging high entrance fees and limiting access via park-run tour buses, as is done in many international parks. While this may be good for some of the species inside the parks, it can be bad news for local people who relied on providing horse rides and lodging to tourists as a source of income. In addition, it can increase rates of cultural disruption, as many of the people living near these parks are ethnic minorities. Such practices demonstrate awareness of the commercial value of ecotourism on the part of national and local leaders. In general, Chinese tourists tend to be interested in spectacular waterfalls or rock formations that resemble mythical creatures and provide good photo opportunities rather than in solitary hiking or encounters with wildlife. Getting a photo of oneself standing in front of a famous spot is often the main goal of such visits. Meanwhile, some of China's wildlife managers' approaches to biodiversity tend toward wildlife farms and even cloning (as in the case of the giant panda), rather than preservation of habitat. Tellingly, Jonathan Watts (2010b) cites tales of welcome banquets at nature reserves where the menu features endangered species.

Chinese environmental law dates to 1979 and the beginning of the post-Mao reform era, when the Environmental Protection Law of the People's Republic of China laid out responsibilities for pollution prevention and resource use. It established basic institutions, giving the Ministry of Construction (now Ministry of Housing and Urban-Rural

Development) an environmental portfolio. It articulated "three magic weapons": environmental impact assessments, liability for polluters through pollution discharge fees, and the "three synchronizations" policy, which required implementation of pollution control measures during the "design, construct, and operate" phases of a project (Sinkule and Ortolano 1995). The early environmental protection bureaucracy became the State Environmental Protection Administration (SEPA) in 1998, and did not become the cabinet-level Ministry of Environmental Protection (MEP) until 2008. It is still widely viewed as a weak institution compared with other long-established ministries with broad portfolios.

Nonetheless, the MEP can boast significant achievements, many of them spearheaded by top environmental leader Qu Geping, who is often considered the father of China's environmental protection. In 1993, Qu persuaded many government departments to support a national media campaign to expose polluters and clean up the environment. Prior to this time, the media had avoided environmental issues for fear of appearing anti-socialist. Reporters then began to ferret out and publicize the names of polluters and their factories. The number of stories about the environment during the first seven years of the media campaign totaled 50,000. The press called it a "green hurricane" cleaning up China. Tens of thousands of the worst factories were closed. However, pollution continued to build. Environmental damage was criminalized in the mid-1990s, and in 1994, the first environmental groups were allowed to form (about which more later). One of Qu's most important contributions was the passage of the 2004 Environmental Impact Assessment Law. A key feature was a provision that allowed ordinary citizens to participate in the governmental assessment of major projects, like dams, that would have a significant environmental impact. The law, which requires developers to obtain approval from the Ministry of Environmental Protection before proceeding, has been difficult to enforce because some developers, including major power companies like Huaneng and Huadian Power, have often forged ahead without permits. These companies have been willing to pay the relatively small fines from the MEP rather than wait for approval.

Since then, many new environmental standards and regulations have been issued, providing a sophisticated and credible framework for achieving resource protection and pollution prevention. However, none garnered the level of public interest and excitement as the new environmental protection laws that went into effect in January 2015, the first major change to the legislation in 25 years. Now with 70 articles instead of only 47 in the 1989 version, the revised laws require that economic and social development be coordinated with environmental protection. Other highlights include a daily accumulative penalty for repeat polluters (earlier fines were so light that factories often budgeted for them as a cost of doing business) and an exciting new component that permits environmental public interest litigation. Although many argue that the enforceability of these stringent clauses is still in question, it is clear that the laws will have more "teeth" than in the past.

The content of the new environmental law has been widely discussed and debated, but equally significant is the legislative process by which it came into being. Two rounds of month-long public consultation elicited more than 14,000 comments from more than 10,000 individuals and organizations. In yet another encouraging sign for public participation, the law gives civil society a chapter for the first time, stating that a citizen has the right to access environmental information, and to participate in and monitor activities relating to environmental protection. As Greenpeace's China program director Ma Tianjie writes in the *South China Morning Post*,

Chinese society has tremendous expectations for this new law. Three years in the making, the revision process itself speaks volumes about the stakes involved. The public-interest litigation clause alone triggered a highly publicised, multi-round discussion among ministries, non-governmental organisations and legal scholars that had never been seen in previous legislative processes. But for any law, the devil is always in enforcement. Chinese laws are never short of the so-called "sleeping beauty clauses" – nicely written items that are in reality never enforced, either due to the intrinsic vagueness in the law itself or the unwillingness of law enforcement to trigger them. (Ma 2015)

Since the law was passed, the Supreme Court has issued several judicial interpretations on environmental public interest litigation and established a special environmental tribunal, and the Ministry of Environmental Protection has released detailed regulations to guide the local enforcement process. As Zhang Bo and Cao Cong (2015) write in *Nature*, "Effective environmental governance needed a new law. Now it requires robust implementation mechanisms, accountability regimes and institutional arrangements." The appointment of rising star Chen Jining as new Environment Minister in early 2015 also stirred public interest, as the prior administration had been perceived as inefficient and often ineffective. Although Chen has no prior government experience, he is former president of Tsinghua University and has strong Party ties.

IMPLEMENTATION CHALLENGES

Overall, implementation of environmental protection laws remains difficult. Indeed, legal scholar Charles McElwee (2011, p. vii) provides a long list of challenges, including: "low status of law as a means of achieving societal goals"; "lack of capacity within the country's bureaucracies and legal institutions"; "delegation of responsibility for environmental protection to local authorities"; "strong influence of informal networks on the application and administration of laws and regulations"; and "structural flaws in existing laws and regulations." The deeper problem, as noted above, is the culture of corruption and lack of confidence in the fair and equal application of law; every rule seems made to be broken. Legal provisions can be vague and enforcement statutes toothless. Powerful officials and businessmen find ways around the regulations, and until recently very few polluters found themselves subject to criminal prosecution. This explains why in practice dams are built after minimal or no environmental impact review. Illegal mines open, and then reopen after authorities shut them down. Real estate developers expropriate farmland and raze entire neighborhoods in the face of fierce resistance and deadly confrontations with residents as a development boom tramples the rights of families who have lived in their homes for generations. The *New York Times* describes the special term the Chinese use to describe the last holdouts' lonely "nail houses" that stand alone when all others have been bulldozed (Wines and Ansfield 2010). Many Chinese dream of the day that there will be "rule of law" rather than "rule by law," and justice will be handed down even to high officials and their "princeling" children. I will never forget hearing a woman whose son had been arrested for a minor infraction ask her friends if anyone knew how to get a gift to the judge. When I lived in China in the early post-Mao years, it was common for people to spend every penny beyond subsistence income on cigarettes, watches, and more expensive bribes for officials who controlled residence permits, housing, salaries, and passports. The same dynamic still operates today and affects the state's ability to implement anti-pollution laws.

Some implementation challenges are structural: the Ministry of Environmental Protection has comparatively little enforcement power. It supervises Environmental Protection Bureaus (EPBs) and Offices in a pyramidal fashion opening downward to the provinces, counties, townships, and so on (some localities did not even have EPBs until the 1990s). However, as political scientist Kenneth Lieberthal (2003) explains, the quasi-federal administrative system in China is a form of fragmented authoritarianism, based on both verticality and horizontality. In China this is known as the *tiao-kuai* [条块], or "branches and lumps" arrangement. Functionally, as in the case of environmental governance, there is a vertical hierarchy, but territorially there is a competing horizontal level of authority held by provincial and local governments. In terms of rank, provincial governments hold status equal to central ministries. Therefore, in practice, central ministries like the MEP cannot issue a binding order to a provincial government. Moreover, local governments are often funded by the same industries that the EPBs are supposed to regulate, leading to all kinds of perverse incentives. Environmental officials are often hired by and beholden to local Party and government leaders and answer to them rather than to their superiors in the environmental bureaucracy. Indeed, local EPBs' budgets, leadership and personnel decisions, as well as decisions to permanently close plants are still made by local governments (Economy 2004), although the 2015 law does grant local EPBs the power to suspend production in factories that violate standards. Local officials have been given great power to implement central government goals of both economic growth and environmental protection, but in cases where the goals conflict, they tend to favor growth and industrial activity. Because of their weak structural position, local EPBs must often obtain permission from the local government to close down enterprises. Some corrupt EPB officials are linked to mayors and Party chiefs and may even participate in the revenues from small-scale factories or mines either directly or through complex networks of relatives and friends. Local protectionism at the village level is rampant. While so-called Township and Village Enterprises (TVEs) have often been blamed for much of China's pollution, they have also been a lifeline for local peasants to escape grueling farm work and provided towns and regions with important revenue (Jahiel 1997; 1998; Ma and Ortolano 2000).

Another complication for the MEP is that of bureaucratic overlap and contradiction in the central government apparatus. Other ministries such as the Ministry of Commerce have mandates to promote economic growth, while environmental issues like the governance of rivers and lakes, including water use rights and pollution, are handled not only by the Ministry of Water Resources but also by regional river commissions as well as other ministries. Key environmental problems affecting farmland, such as erosion, salinization, heavy metals pollution, and desertification, fall under the aegis of the Ministry of Agriculture but are also under the domain of the Ministry of Land and Resources and MEP. There are competing and conflicting emphases on growth, government legitimacy, clean development, and stability, creating a confusing policy-making landscape in which actors sometimes work at cross purposes or with uncertain lines of responsibility. Moreover, the emphasis on growth has filtered down into the entire Party-State apparatus, so that when local officials are evaluated for promotion, they tend to be rewarded for spearheading economic activity rather than for protecting the environment. Efforts are being made to change this calculus with rewards for environmental protection as well as growth, but success varies greatly from region to region and even from city to city. The result is that some cities, like Xiamen and Dalian (ironically, the site of the oil spill mentioned in a previous chapter), have reputations as particularly "green," while coal-rich cities like Linfen and Taiyuan in Shanxi are famed for the intensity of their coal dust and air and water pollution.

Economic realities and concerns about unemployment and social unrest often push the government away from environmentally friendly action. The Ministry of Environmental Protection is hardly in a position to close the enormous state-run iron and steel plants in the great northeastern rust belt, as unemployment is exceedingly high and shutdowns would mean even more job losses. To make matters more difficult, China is, in effect, sitting on a mountain of cheap coal, one of the dirtiest of fossil fuels. To expect China not to exploit this resource, or to exploit it only with the most up-to-date modern scrubbers or expensive carbon capture and sequestration technologies (a method of reintroducing the carbon into the earth that is under discussion in developed countries) is unrealistic at best, and seems to be asking China to act in a manner more responsible than that of the developed world. Encouragingly, China is moving to ban the import of coal with high ash and sulfur content, although this is a worrisome move for some trading partners like Australia. In 2014, Chinese coal consumption actually dropped for the first time.

Given clear disincentives to move away from the heavy reliance on coal, several Chinese cities, including Beijing, are experimenting with pilot carbon trading schemes, a development that other countries are watching with great interest. China plans to combine these projects and launch the largest carbon trading market in the world some time in 2016. The Chinese seem to be looking for win-win solutions that both alleviate the particulate pollution that causes so much misery and poor health within its borders while going at least part of the way toward addressing the CO_2 emissions causing dangerous climate change in the global atmosphere; such solutions are often discussed in terms of "co-benefits." They have also poured money into greenbelt projects intended to hold the line on creeping desertification, the source of so many sandstorms, while also serving as carbon "sinks."

The government has partnered with industry to provide powerful incentives to develop renewable energy technologies, which now play significant roles in China's economy both domestically and in the export market (Mastny 2010). China is a major global competitor in markets like solar and wind energy; in 2010 it became the world's largest provider of wind turbines. According to figures from the state-run *Xinhua* news agency, the country installed nearly 18 GW of new wind power in 2011 bringing total wind power capacity to 62.4 GW. Unfortunately, about one-quarter of this is not connected to the grid. While this is only a tiny fraction of the country's total energy mix, recent studies have shown that the potential for Chinese wind power is enormous. Wind power alone could supply all of China's power needs for the next 20 years if it were fully developed (Fairley 2009). As for solar, the 2011 bankruptcy and closure of solar manufacturers in the United States put China well ahead of other countries in solar technology and export. In 2013 China became the world's leading installer of photovoltaics, with 400 companies and capacity double that of the year before. However, capacity expansion in "green" industry sometimes comes at a high cost. By analyzing the carbon footprint and energy usage involved in making solar panels, researchers found the environmental cost of Chinese-made solar panels is about twice that of those made in Europe, leaving a "dirty cost" for a green industry (Ramzy 2014). In the automotive sector, the government is investing billions of dollars in hybrid and electric vehicles with the intention of becoming the world leader in manufacturing greener cars. China is now the world's largest automobile market, surpassing the U.S. in 2011, but unfortunately, despite government efforts, consumers seem less interested in "green" cars than in sport utility vehicles, according to a report in the *Guardian* by Jonathan Watts (2011). It will be important to see whether government and corporate persuasion can shift that perception and turn energy-efficient cars into status symbols.

Some Chinese scholars and policy makers have not been shy to confront the problems of achieving sustainable development. We have already noted high-ranking environmental leader Qu Geping's famous book on population and the environment in China. Among other top leaders, then-State Science and Technology Commission head Song Jian was proactive in mobilizing China's attention to environmental issues in advance of the 1992 Rio U.N. Conference on Environment and Development (UNCED). The most critical of the scholarly Chinese analyses is undoubtedly the influential 1998 book, *Grave Concerns: Problems of Sustainable Development in China* by two Chinese Academy of Social Sciences Environmental and Development Institute researchers, Zheng Yisheng and Qian Yihong (a link to a summary translation in English is at the end of this chapter). Their analysis understands the barriers to sustainable development as largely political, including poor coordination among bureaucratic agencies and between the center and local governments, as well as lack of implementation of environmental laws and regulations. Zheng and Qian argue that there are deep structural problems such as the collective property rights system under which land is not privately held, corruption, and failure to respect individual rights and laws which will make it difficult for China to achieve its goals. While we may wish to debate their notion that privatization will solve China's environmental problems, we must admire their willingness to challenge such core principles of socialism. Even today, the Party holds to the fiction that land in private hands is being leased and ultimately belongs to the state, which creates many gray areas in the economy and a state of uncertainty about whether resources will be available to landholders in the future. Those who favor privatization argue that certainty over land tenure would promote sustainable use for the long term.

Other measures to improve the country's environmental performance include a typically Chinese central government approach to social change: creating "model environmental cities." This is a throwback of sorts to the Maoist practice of finding model individuals or places that others are supposed to emulate. During the Cultural Revolution, agriculture was supposed to "learn from" the backbreaking work of the Dazhai production brigade, industry to "learn from" the iron man spirit of the Daqing oilfields, and model soldiers, workers, and peasants were glorified on postage stamps with ordinary citizens being made to "study" their lives. Many of these models were manufactured for propaganda purposes, which may explain why people nowadays tend to be skeptical of such campaigns. However, cities can benefit by competing for National Model City status, which they can then use to promote tourism, draw investment, and host international events, as the formerly dirty city of Shenyang did when attracting a horticultural exhibition. There have been numerous competitions and public ceremonies recognizing not only cities but also model industries and leading individuals. A prominent example is the eco-city being built near Tianjin with the help of the government of Singapore. Not all such efforts succeed – the highly publicized eco-city of Dongtan near Shanghai was never built, a fantasy that evaporated in corruption and poor planning (Sze 2015). Of course, there is always a risk that in applying for model status a city will simply force polluting industries to relocate beyond city limits, which is in effect what happened when Beijing cleaned up its air in preparation for the 2008 Olympics and for the 2014 APEC summit. Still, the effort to find a pattern that works and then replicate it in other cities may be a useful way to encourage wider adoption of best practices, as long as local conditions are also respected and the model is not imposed dogmatically. During the Mao period, a model was taken to an extreme when the labor-intensive hillside terraces of Dazhai were imposed throughout the country, resulting in disastrous erosion in areas where slopes were too steep for the terraces or the terrain otherwise unsuited (Shapiro 2001).

The Chinese government's struggle to regulate its vast and complex society can be illustrated by the widespread incidence of lead poisoning from battery factories and smelters, the subject of a 2011 report by U.S.-based Human Rights Watch. Villagers in severely contaminated towns have faced stonewalling by local government officials, misinformation about testing and treatment, cover-ups, and government failure to shut down factories with egregious environmental violations. The *New York Times* told the story of one village in Zhejiang where large numbers of adults and children were found to have up to seven times the safe level of lead in their blood. A mob of 200 people rioted in the Zhejiang Haijun Battery Factory, smashing filing cabinets and windows in an outpouring of rage designed to get the government to pay attention (LaFraniere 2011).

The scandals around melamine additives in infant formula and milk powder, although they do not directly involve the environmental bureaucracy, illustrate the Chinese government's lack of power to supervise industrial practices. Melamine, a fertilizer additive, artificially boosts the nitrogen content of milk, thereby giving a false reading of higher protein content. Beginning in 2008, melamine was discovered as an illegal additive in milk powder and infant formula. In March of that year, an unusually high number of cases of infant kidney stones caught the attention of Nanjing Children's Hospital and from March to September, the incidence of kidney problems in infants surged. Doctors discovered that most of them had been fed formula produced by the Sanlu Group, a major dairy company based in Shijiazhuang in Hebei Province. Despite complaints from consumers and an increasing number of sick infants, and even after government authorities detected melamine in infant formula on July 24, Sanlu continued to sell melamine-contaminated milk powder until it was recalled on September 11. By December 2008 almost 300,000 infants had been made sick and six died. In January 2009, the former chairwoman of the Sanlu Group was sentenced to life imprisonment. November saw the execution of Geng Jinping and Zhang Yujun, two main producers and sellers of hundreds of tons of melamine-containing "albumin powder" that had been added to raw milk.

Amazingly, despite the national scandal and international loss of face, the strong government response, the overhaul of the overly complex and overlapping food safety regulatory system, and the increases in inspections, the problem has not definitively been resolved (Yan 2013). After sweeping shutdowns of thousands of small food producers, in part for industrial restructuring but also to improve inspection capacity, 26 more metric tons of contaminated milk powder were confiscated, as recently as April 2011. Understandably, Chinese parents are now willing to pay high premiums for products imported from the West for their children, while top government officials in

Beijing get their food from contracted farms whose products are guaranteed to be safe. One of the most popular purchases by Chinese tourists traveling abroad is Western-produced vitamin supplements, which are believed to be safer and more effective than those manufactured at home. I have seen Chinese visitors spend hundreds of dollars on these. Unfortunately, in 2013 the discovery of the heavy metal cadmium in rice produced in Hunan, one of China's most prolific agricultural provinces, did little to reassure consumers that their food supply was safe.

Government ineffectuality was also on display after a new bullet train fell off a bridge in July 2011, when the government tried to force the media to report heartwarming stories about a rescued infant rather than about the people who were killed. In reaction to the public outcry, the state announced a temporary halt to new high-speed train projects, although construction has since entered again into full-throttle mode. In recent years, Chinese courts have sentenced to death more than a few agency heads, mayors, and factory leaders charged with responsibility for industrial accidents and flagrant safety violations. However, such sentences and crackdowns speak to the government's need to be perceived as taking action rather than to the prospect that an airtight system of inspection and enforcement will soon be in place. The central Chinese government's response to scandals about accidents and toxicity is all too often damage control, denial, and counter-accusations.

These efforts are top-down measures that fail to empower Chinese consumers to act upon their indignation. If China is to correct its dangerous consumer product and public safety situation, there must be improved access to information through honest labeling, as well as a legal system capable of redressing harm and enabling Chinese citizens to gain oversight over public health and safety (challenges, admittedly, for developed countries as well). To date, Chinese consumers and victims of public health hazards have few avenues for redress other than taking to the streets and calling government complaint lines. Such actions occasionally meet with success, but more often are suppressed or ignored. By Chinese law, consumers are legally entitled to recoup fourfold the price of a defective product or service, thanks to a new consumer protection law that came into effect in March 2014 but which is still inadequate. Moreover, the class-action lawsuit is underutilized and poorly understood as a consumer protection tool, and it is difficult to get courts to accept such cases.

Lead, melamine, and other food and industrial scandals show us clearly that governance involves far more than government – regulations, laws, and legal deterrents have not been adequate to prevent behavior where the profit motive is so much stronger than the risk of discovery, and where ethical standards have become so confused. Indeed, these examples are just two of many failures of the Chinese system to protect citizens. Accidents in construction, transport, mining, and industry are also common; factory fires and explosions are everyday events. As a Chinese blogger pled eloquently after the bullet train crash, "China, please stop your flying pace, wait for your people, wait for your soul, wait for your morality, wait for your conscience! Don't let the train run out of track, don't let the bridges collapse, don't let the roads become traps, don't let houses become ruins. Walk slowly, allowing every life to have freedom and dignity. No one should be left behind by our era." As reported in the *New York Times* (Johnson 2011), this blogger captures the fact that China's out-of-control development and growth shake the nation's very identity. Ecologists tell us that ecosystems can adapt if changes occur slowly, but when environmental tipping points are reached, cascading events can cause the whole system to collapse. With its fast pace of growth and lack of regulatory control, China seems to be flirting with these thresholds.

As we have seen in this chapter, the Chinese government cannot simply say the word and implement a law or policy. Governance, even in an authoritarian country, is a messy process and a policy or law on paper is not the same as achieving widespread compliance. This is especially true where state regulatory capacity is weak and non-compliance is seen as normal, and where the government weakens its own capacity through conflicting priorities like maintaining economic growth and limiting unemployment and social unrest. Fortunately, other institutions, including citizens' groups, are now taking a role in influencing public behavior toward the environment, and exerting pressure despite the government's fear of what might happen if it made pollution and accident information more transparent. Before we turn to this rich topic, however, we need to better understand some of the historical and cultural factors that complicate China's efforts to achieve sustainable development. While we do not want to make too much of the role of national culture in diplomatic (or undiplomatic) behavior, and while not all scholars believe that political culture explains very much, in the next chapter we will explore the notion that there is a link between culture and the prospects for sustainability, not only in China but everywhere.

QUESTIONS FOR RESEARCH AND DISCUSSION

1 Given the overlapping and competing mandates of Chinese government bureaucracies, what needs to change to support better environmental governance? How can we explain the disconnections among law, policy, regulation, implementation, and enforcement in the Chinese case?

2 How should we understand the interactions among the many factors that contribute to environmental degradation? Are some factors more fundamental or difficult to deal with than others? What would sustainable development in China look like?

3 What might be some of the Chinese government's motivations in stressing sustainable development and environmental protection?

Should the government merely reflect the values of the citizenry, or does the government have a responsibility to lead the Chinese people toward more sustainable behavior? Do you think the government's policies recognize values of sustainability such as public health, well-being, and justice?

4 What should China's role in international environmental politics be? How do the country's policy makers see their responsibilities under various environmental treaties? Is China's position on climate change reasonable?

ADDITIONAL RESOURCES

- *China Daily*, "Green China" blog, available at: http://www.chinadaily.com.cn/bizchina/greenchina/index.html
- U.S. Environmental Protection Agency's China Environmental Law Initiative, at: http://www.epa.gov/ogc/china/initiative_home.htm
- Congressional-Executive Commission on China, at: www.cecc.gov
- Ministry of Environmental Protection (MEP) official English-language website, at: http://english.mep.gov.cn/
- U.S.-Asia Partnerships for Environmental Law, at: http://www.vermontlaw.edu/academics/environmental_law_center/institutes_and_initiatives/us-china_partnership_for_environmental_law/overview.htm
- Zheng Yisheng and Qian Yihong (1998) "China's Environment, Politics and the Economy: Grave Concerns." Link to U.S. Embassy-Beijing translation: http://gaodawei.wordpress.com/2011/04/09

4 | Sustainable Development and National Identity _____

What are the cultural and historical contexts in which China is trying to achieve sustainable development, and how do they affect the prospects for success? We saw in the last chapter that, at least in its rhetoric, China's stated public commitment to sustainable development is strong. Implementation shortfalls notwithstanding, the government has integrated sustainability into its five-year plans, passed laws mandating an ambitious national renewable energy portfolio, invested in research and development for green technologies and clean air and water initiatives, and participated actively in international discussions of global environmental challenges. However, China's prospects for achieving sustainable development are clouded by a political system that restricts public participation in environmental decision making, a political culture of insecurity, and uncertainty over national identity at a time of enormous economic growth and social change.

National identity can be understood as encompassing core values, world views, and self-understood history. It includes interpretations of where a given people stand at the present moment, as well as future dreams, goals, and ambitions for the destiny of the nation. National identity is socially constructed and malleable (Anderson 1983); it is contested by different social groups and manipulated by the state, which controls the official version of history. In China, for example, the birth and triumph of the Chinese Communist Party are celebrated, but the excesses and ideological extremism of the Cultural Revolution are absent from textbooks, while public debate about its causes is stifled.

The state decides which holidays to celebrate. China marks political holidays such as October 1st, National Day; after Mao Zedong's death the Party relaxed restrictions on traditional festivals such as the Dragon Boat Festival that marks the drowning of the poet Chu Yuan and the Qingming day of reverence for ancestors, thereby signaling that it was distancing itself from the Mao-era characterization of all traditional culture as feudal. The state decides which symbols to use on currency, as when it sent a strong message reasserting the legacy of Mao by putting his face on the reissued 100 *yuan* and other notes in 1999. As the great anthropologist Clifford Geertz (1973) has taught, national identity is bound up in values and world views that are captured through public symbols and rituals and which give citizens a sense of their connection to their communities and the meaning of their lives. These are all things that the state attempts to control, with varied success; many Han Chinese are skeptical about the official version of history, and non-Han minorities even more so.

Most of China's 55 recognized non-Han minority ethnic groups (comprising about one-tenth of the population) have different narratives, values, and traditions, despite the official version of Chinese history that touts the integrity of Chinese geopolitical borders and the long, unbroken history of the Chinese people. In fact, China's state-building process has been far messier and more complex. Territorial borders have shifted dramatically since the time of the "unifying emperor" Qinshi Huangdi (259–210 BC) and China has twice been ruled by foreign dynasties. The country's present-day border disputes are only now being resolved, with parts of the long border with India still heavily contested. The state has enshrined an uneasy, essentially colonial relationship with frontier peoples. It has done so through the establishment of "autonomous" regions, counties, and towns intended to provide a modicum of self-government and self-determination; through the creation of Minorities Institutes, which are universities and research centers that train minority elites while enshrining and studying local cultural traditions; and by providing preferential treatment in birth quotas and designating spots for minorities in elite schools. Meanwhile, among the Han, minorities are often stereotyped as lazy, dirty, and exotic, unlike the official version, which shows China and its minorities as one big happy family. Woe to the ethnic minority group that seeks to challenge that narrative.

This chapter argues that the Chinese people are in essence in the throes of a crisis of identity, in which the nation is simultaneously well aware of its world prominence in past Imperial times and of its more recent humiliation at the hands of foreign powers from the mid-19th to mid-20th centuries. This dynamic can be understood, perhaps a bit crudely, as a "superiority-inferiority complex."

On the "superiority" side, there is a proud conviction that in prior millennia China was a great, unified Han civilization. China was the center of civilization, more advanced than other lands, a "Middle Kingdom" (the literal meaning of the Chinese characters for China, *zhongguo* 中国), where an emperor with the Mandate of Heaven to rule enjoyed tribute from other nations whose representatives traveled great distances to the Court to demonstrate their respect. This great Chinese civilization fostered the ancient philosophical traditions of Confucianism, Buddhism, and Daoism, among others, all of which articulated high moral values and offered prescriptions for achieving self-cultivation and a harmonious society. With regard to the non-human world, these traditions offered wisdom about the sustainable use of natural resources, reverence for all forms of life, and living in accordance with nature's flow (Weller 2006). Chinese are taught in school that they invented gunpowder, dynamite, the printing press, the compass, and paper, among thousands of other scientific innovations (all well chronicled by the great Sinologist Joseph Needham in his epic 27-volume work, *Science and Civilization in China*); their textbooks often start with the discovery of Peking Man as the first human being and key to a Marxist scientific outlook (Schmalzer 2008). Through their innovations in building complex waterworks projects, some of which survive to this day, the ancient Chinese harnessed nature by developing centralized political systems that facilitated social organization and flood control. The German Sinologist Karl Wittfogel (1957) even hypothesized, too simplistically perhaps, that the level of centralization required for such irrigation projects in "hydraulic societies" explains the emergence of the Chinese dynastic imperial system. Nonetheless, Yu the Great, the legendary founding emperor of the Xia Dynasty (about 2100 BC), is said to have gained his power and legitimacy by taming the waters during a great flood, cutting irrigation canals into the earth in place of failed dykes, and creating massive irrigation works, as in the historical tale, "Yu the Great controls the waters" [Da Yu zhishui 大禹治水]. In later years, Mao situated himself squarely within this tradition, building multiple dams and dreaming of blocking the Three Gorges on the Yangzi River. Mastery of nature has thus been a consistent part of the narrative of state power from prehistory, establishing a link between dynastic legitimacy and control of resources.

Most Chinese are ruefully aware, however, that somewhere along the way their great civilization lost this advantage, becoming known throughout the world as the "sick man of Asia," or as the founding father of modern China, Sun Yat-sen, famously put it in 1924, "a pile of loose sand," vulnerable to depredations and incursions of imperialist powers. This equally significant element of Chinese national identity thus tells the more recent history of humiliation at the hands of foreign powers. Indeed, the final dynasty, the Qing (1644–1911), was not Han but Manchu, a minority people from what is today Northeast China.

The events of the "centuries of humiliation" are sometimes treated as if they occurred yesterday. The Chinese were forced to import opium after the Opium Wars of the mid-19th century, with the concomitant problems of dependency and addiction, because the trade was highly lucrative for the British and other foreign powers who exchanged opium for Chinese tea. These wars were followed by a series of "unequal treaties" the Chinese were forced to sign in the 19th and early 20th centuries. Imposed by foreign powers after military defeat, they induced the Chinese to give up valuable land such as Hong Kong and Macao (to the British and Portuguese, respectively), to open their ports to foreign trade, to permit foreign missionaries to proselytize, and to allow foreign nationals to be subject not to Chinese law but to foreign legal systems while living in China. The centuries of humiliation also included the Russian invasion of Manchuria in the Northeast in 1900 and the carving of the great city of Shanghai into colonial fiefdoms, where elegant parts of town were off limits to Chinese. After the fall of the Qing dynasty in 1911, some of the unequal treaties with European colonial powers were abrogated. But the country descended into regional warlordism and a debilitating, multi-phase civil war between the Communists (CCP) and Nationalists (Kuomintang or KMT, or Guomindang or GMD depending on the Romanization system). This internal strife continued even during the invasion of China by Japan, the "rape" of the city of Nanjing in 1937, and the flight of both Nationalist and Communist armies toward the interior. When the Japanese were defeated in 1945, the civil war flared anew. Understandably, the Communist victory in 1949 was widely celebrated, with its promise of peace and prosperity. Mao's famous proclamation, as he stood on the reviewing stand at Tiananmen Square, "The Chinese people have stood up!" symbolized the passionate aspirations of the Chinese people.

A Communist Youth League instructor once lectured me for hours about the sins of foreign colonial powers. I had the misfortune to be berthed opposite him on an overnight train in Sichuan Province. He seemed to hold me personally responsible for the evils of my imperialist forebears, despite my protestations that I had not been born when any of these things happened, nor had my ancestors been involved in Asia. It was a good opportunity for me to see what every Chinese student is taught in mandatory "theory" and "Party history" classes in high school and university, and to understand why resentment toward foreigners may still lurk just beneath the surface of otherwise hospitable interactions.

Since those years of humiliation, China has struggled to reclaim what it regards as its rightful place at the center of the world. There is thus great sensitivity to indications of respect and rank. A preoccupation with "face" and status lies at the core of the tension between superiority and inferiority in Chinese national identity; the country's position in the eyes of the world is a primary concern for China and its citizens. This prickliness to questions of "face" arguably governs at least some of the country's international behavior. Memories of national humiliation at the hands of foreign powers can induce hair-trigger reactions to perceived slights (Gries 2005). Aggressive nationalism flares up easily, as is seen in competition against other nations for claims to ocean resources in the South China Sea, the Sea of Japan, and the East China Sea, which China recently proclaimed to be "core interests" along with Taiwan and Tibet.

This preoccupation underlay the delirium of national happiness when China was awarded the 2008 Olympics after many failed bids, and it helps explain the government's nervousness about air quality and the weather on opening night. So determined was the central government that the Olympics would mark China's great coming-out party on the world stage that it invested great sums to train athletes to win gold medals, even in sports where China had no prior tradition. It mobilized thousands of song and dance troupe members for years of preparation for the most lavish opening ceremonies in history The focus on reputation and status plays into China's desire to build the world's tallest, fanciest, most innovative and expensive buildings. Architects adore receiving Chinese commissions, for it seems there is no limit on imagination or cost, and buildings like the Bird's Nest stadium have won prizes throughout the world. (Embarrassingly, however, Rem Koolhaas' 2008 CCTV edifice has been nicknamed "the big underpants" for its two-legged design.) The Chinese are building the world's fastest trains, longest bridges, and most modern airports. The preoccupation with China's reputation contributes to the investment in the space program and the emphasis on putting a man on the moon, even at a time when rural children's parents struggle to pay school fees and Mao-era safety nets for workers and retirees have all but disappeared. National pride helps explain why China persisted in building the Three Gorges Dam at a time when developed countries were rethinking the wisdom of megaprojects that so dramatically alter the natural environment. "Face" also helps to explain why the Chinese reacted with outrage in 1995 when American environmentalist Lester Brown's book *Who Will Feed China?* raised concerns about the global grain supply. The Chinese even published a rebuttal called "China Will Feed China," as if it were an insult to imply that China could not be self-reliant in grain (in fact, China's increasing reliance on the international grain market has had an impact on food prices, which is being felt painfully in the world's poorest countries, as basic foodstuffs become increasingly expensive).

In international forums, sensitivity over "face" may explain why Chinese negotiators temporarily left the 2009 Copenhagen round of climate change negotiations in a huff when they discovered they had not been included in some side events, as well as the effort they put into placing a Chinese among the top officials at the International Monetary Fund when the 2011 arrest of Dominique Strauss-Kahn appeared to provide an opening at the top leadership (they won a number three spot). It may help explain China's active efforts to improve its poor reputation as an international investor that disregards the environment and vulnerable communities in Southeast Asia, Africa, and Latin America. Preoccupation with face may also motivate some of China's behavior toward the Republic of China, Taiwan. China has provided generous aid to some of the world's smallest countries when they agreed to renege on their recognition of Taiwan. China even blocked membership for Taiwan in the World Health Organization despite the fact that Taiwan, along with Hong Kong and Guangdong, was at the center of the major SARS virus outbreak in 2003. (Taiwan gained observer status at the WHO governing body in 2009.) The principle of a united China also plays a role in these efforts to regain past glory and reassert the Communist Party's defeat of the Kuomintang once and for all. The return of Hong Kong to China from British rule in 1997, one of the last vestiges of the unequal treaties, was marked with year-long, government-orchestrated celebrations, including per-formances, special souvenirs, lavish propaganda, and public demon-strations of apparently sincere patriotic joy. This has since been complicated by Hong Kong residents' 2014 "umbrella revolution" to protect the "one country, two systems" promises that China would not interfere with the democratic system the British left behind.

CHINESE PHILOSOPHICAL TRADITIONS

Chinese identity is, of course, far more complex than a matter of face. Indeed, to the extent that national culture usually involves some account of the human relationship to the non-human world, some Chinese environmentalists believe that traditional Chinese culture's elements of sustainability may provide important guidance during the current spiritual crisis of disillusionment and materialism. Their task is to create an ethical justification for a home-grown environmentalism. It must make sense in the Chinese context and not simply appear to be a Western import intended to prevent China from developing, as some government policy makers suspect and suggest. All three major ancient traditions have themes related to what we now call sustainabil-ity. Confucianism does so from an anthropocentric, or human-centered environmental perspective; Buddhism from a biocentric, or life-cen-tered perspective; and Daoism from an ecocentric, or ecosystem-cen-tered perspective (Weller 2006). Interestingly, Western environmental traditions have a similar range of philosophical approaches. The "stewardship" mandate of the Judeo-Christian tradition is human centered; the humane compassion of those who protect animals from cruelty and exploitation is rooted in reverence for the lives of all individual beings. The eco-centered land ethic guides conservation biologists and leads them to protect the world's "last great places," "critical eco-regions," "biogems," and "biodiversity hotspots" (in phrases used by the Nature Conservancy, World Wide Fund for Nature, Natural Resources Defense Council, and Conservation International).

Many of China's ethnic minorities also have a history of stewardship and protection of the land. "Sacred groves," "sacred mountains," and sacred lakes" are de facto protected areas where biodiversity flourishes. All the more destructive of local culture, then, are the Han incursions for mining, hydropower, and mass tourism. The Naxi minority, for example, who number about 300,000 and live in Yunnan Province in Southwest China, have a deep tradition of reverence for nature and a strict code that governs the use of water and harvesting of trees. Many of their forests were cut down during the Great Leap Forward and religious practices were banned during the Cultural Revolution. In one of the old ceremonies kept alive by religious leaders, prayers and offerings are made to the god of nature, asking to be forgiven for the damage to nature in daily life. If water and trees are not protected, it is believed, bad things such as floods, diseases, and crop failures will result.

In ancient China, as reflected in today's Communist Party's stated goal to achieve a "Harmonious Society," sociopolitical harmony in the human world was the most important social value. Orderly hierarchical relationships were bedrocks of the dominant Confucian tradition (and may underlie some of the preoccupation with respect and status described above). Such classics as the *Analects* teach moral qualities that promote both good leadership and loyalty. Rank and role, correctly performed, are the basis for social order. The correct performance of loyalty to one's superiors is amply repaid with paternalistic protection

(Evasdottir 2004). Yet despite the focus on human relationships and such core values as filial piety, benevolence, ritual, morality, and loyalty [*xiao, ren, li, de, zhong* 孝,仁,礼,德,忠], Confucianism also provides sensible precepts like protecting spawning fish and refraining from hunting in spring when animals are young. Raising freshwater prawn in rice paddies and carp in pools, as has been done in China for millennia, is often cited as one of the earliest examples of a sustainable and efficient farming system.

Chinese Buddhism (one of many schools of Buddhism, which is practiced differently in Sri Lanka, India, Tibet, Mongolia, Korea, Japan, and elsewhere), retains the notion of reincarnation of souls. Chinese Buddhist monks and nuns are often vegetarian, and many devout practitioners visit temples to have a vegetarian meal. On some festival days, Buddhists will purchase and release a bird, fish, or turtle as a way of gaining merit and as an acknowledgement of the connection among living beings and the desire to practice loving kindness to animals. There is thus a close relationship between nature and morality, with compassion to others held as one of the most important virtues. Tibetan Buddhism is even more careful about non-interference with nature, with its many sacred lakes and mountains and belief that cutting into the earth for mining violates the earth gods and that hunting animals for more than subsistence creates bad karma. Tibetan Buddhism has particular appeal for some Han Chinese environmentalists, a few of whom have converted, as depicted in the short film "Searching for Sacred Mountain" (Marcuse 2014).

Daoism, the most metaphysical of the three traditions, is famous for the saying, "the way that can be named is not the eternal way" [*dao ke dao, fei chang dao* 道可道，非常道]. It emphasizes the relationship between humans and the cosmos and sees man as a microcosm of nature, with the energetic *qi* [气], or life-force, flowing throughout the universe. Concepts of balance, the yin and the yang, and action through non-action are associated with this often-mystical school with many roots in folk traditions. Famously, the tradition discusses the power of *wuwei* [无为], or doing nothing. Compared with Confucianism and Buddhism, it most closely approximates ecological thinking, which also studies the flow of energy through ecosystems within the discipline of bioenergetics.

By contrast with these three ancient traditions, a fourth philosophical influence, more powerful by far, has come to dominate the developed world, including China, since the industrial revolution. Western-style modernization, which seeks to master nature through technological innovation, posits a separation between the human and non-human world and views nature as a force to be tamed. Some have seen this as an extension of a Judeo-Christian approach separating humans from nature, as articulated most famously in a 1967 essay by Lynn T. White, Jr., "The historical roots of our ecological crisis." In response to White's essay, some Christians plumbed the Bible for its environmental wisdom, using examples such as "Song of Songs" and the story of St. Francis of Assisi to find inspiration within the tradition (Hessel and Ruether 2000). In China, ironically, the modernization ethos received its starkest expression during the Maoist period, dominated by the slogan, "Man Must Conquer Nature" [*ren ding sheng tian* 人定胜天], which led to endless human suffering and destruction of wetlands and rainforests, and cast nature as an enemy to be humbled and punished (Shapiro 2001).

BIODIVERSITY AND ANIMAL WELFARE

Let us shift now for a moment to consider an example of how Chinese traditional values and practices influence present-day trends. This is particularly clear when we consider threats to biodiversity and the harsh treatment of animals, both domestically and overseas. A classic saying about the people of Guangzhou is that they will eat anything that has four legs except a table. But Cantonese cuisine is just the most obvious example of how traditional Chinese preferences can increase pressure on endangered species. The close association between food and medicine is well established and deeply rooted in ancient historical study and practice. In addition to the use of herbs, acupuncture, and movement practices like Tai Qi and Qigong that do not have negative environmental impacts, Traditional Chinese Medicine (TCM) makes use of the body parts of endangered mammals and reptiles, as well as also some endangered plants such as ginseng root, which can be shaped like a human being and is considered an aphrodisiac. In TCM, the consumer is often believed to acquire the characteristics of the animal eaten – fierceness, sexual prowess, vigor, longevity, and so on. Traditional Chinese Medicine ingredients include tiger bones and claws, rhinoceros horns, shark fins, and the fetuses, scales, and blood of the less well-known pangolin, a type of scaly anteater whose Southeast Asian population is being decimated for meat and medicine. A broad spectrum of turtle species, including sea turtles, is now disappearing due to demand from the Chinese market. Other less commonly known endangered species used in TCM also include the musk deer, sun bear, and Chinese alligator. In an example of how widespread and arcane this problem can be, an elderly Chinese man from California was convicted in 2014 of smuggling swim bladders from the red-listed Totoaba fish from the Gulf of Mexico, each bladder worth $5,000 in the resale Chinese market and considered a cure for infertility, poor circulation, and skin problems.

Until recently, the high cost of these rare wild animals and plants meant that only the elite could afford them, and their purchase and consumption was often associated with high status, luxury wealth display, gift-giving, and demonstrations of filial piety, often to revered elders in need of a pick-me-up. But the skyrocketing purchasing power of the Chinese middle class has placed extreme pressure on these species, despite China's adherence to the Convention on the

International Trade in Endangered Species (CITES), which China joined in 1981 and which it supports with 22 branch offices. Although CITES is one of the global community's oldest environmental treaties, it is underfunded, under-monitored, and poorly enforced at borders, where customs officials often lack training to differentiate between permitted and illegal goods – there is far more pressure to screen for drugs and illegal immigrants. However, according to the NGO TRAFFIC, which monitors and supports CITES, the illegal trade in such creatures has a global value estimated to be in the hundreds of millions of dollars a year, and is often associated with other, better-known illegal activities.

Not all biodiversity loss associated with traditional Chinese culture is related to food and medicine; ivory has been a favored medium for Chinese carvings and trinkets since the Ming dynasty, albeit less favored than jade; entire tusks can be seen in museums, carved with elaborate scenes of people, pagodas, ships, and latticework. The current decimation of African elephant populations is so grave that experts predict extinction in the wild by 2020 if the situation is not brought under control. However, the slaughter of elephants is closely tied to organized criminal syndicates run out of China that also traffic human beings, trade in drugs, and channel funds to rebel armies and rogue militias; about 70% of the ivory taken from African elephants is destined for China (with the U.S. and its large Asian population the second largest market). Poaching has increased dramatically in areas where Chinese are building roads and other major infrastructure projects (about which more in a later section). In effect, elephant tusks have become the "blood diamonds" of the 21st century; elephant poaching has been tied to the Lord's Resistance Army, where the warlord Joseph Kony has reportedly demanded tusks to help pay for his atrocities, as well as to state-sponsored militias and/or rebel groups in Congo, Sudan, South Sudan, and Uganda. The situation has become so dire that poachers are using helicopters to shoot their prey and chainsaws to remove tusks, and park rangers commonly lose their lives in an effort to defend their charges.

Another example of the pressures that traditional Chinese preferences are exerting on biodiversity is in the fishing industry, where aesthetic and cultural values are promoting the destruction of coral reefs in Southeast Asia and the Pacific. The Chinese favor fish that are alive and colorful (especially the auspicious red), believing them to be fresher. In fact, live fish can fetch five times the price of dead ones. Consumers prefer to purchase living animals in wet markets and select them from tanks in restaurants. Some dishes even require the living fish to be placed directly in hot oil. The Chinese market's impact is particularly intense in the Philippines and Indonesia, where poor fishermen often feel they have little choice but to resort to illegal fishing methods so as to harvest as many fish as possible. These include injecting cyanide directly into polyps, which kills the coral and disorients and half-paralyzes the resident fish, making it easy to net them. The methods also include placing dynamite on the reef, a process that kills most of the fish but allows the harvest of some living ones. The center of the live fish trade is in Hong Kong, where about 30% of the catch is re-exported to China.

Sharks, usually harvested by slicing the fins and throwing the animals into the sea to drown (a technique that allows a vessel to magnify its take) are prized for cartilage that is largely tasteless and supplies texture; claims that it has medicinal properties are specious. Yet shark fin soup remains a high-status delicacy at weddings and expensive restaurants wherever many Chinese live. The trade is so lucrative that a pound of fin can sell for US$300, despite increasingly urgent attention from CITES, which has placed four species on its Appendix II list. With the expansion of Chinese global economic might, shark fishing now has worldwide reach, with coastal Africa particularly vulnerable as poor fishermen see opportunities and new markets. In Tanzania, dolphins are dynamited to use as shark bait, while in Mozambique the fin trade is frightening off the international reef divers drawn to a nascent ecotourism industry (Smith 2013). South Africa is a hub of illegal shark fishing in the region, although Hong Kong is its global center and the Taiwanese mafia is also heavily involved, particularly in Latin America. The ENGO WildAid is featuring basketball star Yao Ming in an anti-finning campaign, about which more in the next chapter. The campaign is having an effect, as awareness of the cruelty of the finning practice, as well as of the ecological impact of removing apex predators from the ocean, seems to be spreading among younger Chinese.

Many species of bears are similarly vulnerable due to their role in TCM. The use of bear bile is mentioned in Chinese medical texts as early as the 7th century. Within China, some 7,000 bears on 200 farms spend their lives in cages, tubes inserted into them to extract bile. Unlike some of the other TCMs that use parts from endangered species, it seems that bear bile does have an efficacious effect on some diseases, although synthetic substitutions do just as well. It is difficult to persuade the Chinese consumer, however, that chemical replacements work, even as they remain persuaded that bile taken from a wild bear is more effective than that tapped from a captive one. Bear bile "farming" and consumption tends to be a domestic issue of concern because of its horrific implications for animal welfare, although, with the decimation of bear populations in China and nearby countries, hunters have shifted as far away as the U.S. There they target American black bears in the Shenandoah, Berkshires, and elsewhere. Although the species is not protected under CITES, the export of bear gall bladders is illegal as it is covered under the Lacey Act. In the U.S., bear bladders are made into medicine or sold whole, often in New York, California, and other states with large Chinese populations. Smugglers have been caught digging ginseng in North America as well, particularly in the Great Smoky Mountains National Park. Meanwhile, an epidemic of rhino horn thefts associated with an Irish ring active in

Asia has struck the museums and private collections of Europe and the UK, with rhino horn worth as much as US$65,000 per kilo on the black market even though it is made of the same keratin as a human fingernail.

Finally, we would be remiss not to note that the Chinese shift toward a meat-based diet, from one where sliced meat was used as a condiment or accent ingredient rather than the main dish, has implications for global croplands conversion, water scarcity, animal welfare, and climate change. We know that every pound of feedlot-produced beef requires seven pounds of grain. From an environmental point of view, meat consumption is a singularly inefficient use of energy, water, and land, while from an animal welfare perspective, it is worse still. China is seeking to "modernize" its meat production system through the introduction of Concentrated Animal Feeding Operations (CAFOs) and other horrors of the developed world and it has also purchased meat and fish suppliers overseas, including the U.S. pork producer Smithfield Foods and rights to some of the offshore fisheries of Peru. These are excellent investments from the Chinese perspective, given the widespread mistrust of domestically produced meats, vegetables, and milk, after a long series of scandals and discoveries of heavy metals and pesticides in everything from rice to tea. It is also a way of compensating for its paucity of arable land and water. As Mark Bittman put it in a New York Times opinion piece, "the Smithfield deal is a land and water grab" (Bittman 2013).

The above examples and trends tell us that traditional Chinese belief systems and aesthetic values, coupled with a newly wealthy middle class with adventurous food tastes in addition to a widespread mistrust of domestically produced food, are a toxic combination for global biodiversity. While climate change may eventually become the final blow, habitat loss, pollution, overharvesting, invasive species, and destructive technologies are already causing a global collapse of life forms (Kolbert 2014). Unfortunately, Chinese consumers are a big part of that story.

THE MAO YEARS AND THEIR LEGACY

We return now to our overview of China's historical legacy and its impact on the environmental challenges of today. Imperial decay, humiliation at the hands of foreign powers, warlordism, Japanese invasion, and civil war were followed in 1949 by the Communist victory, and patriotic Chinese returned to the mainland from around the world to build "New China." Children born during the first years of the revolution were told they were the luckiest people in the world (Liang and Shapiro 1983). But almost 30 years of political upheaval and human and natural catastrophe left China in dire straits. During the 1966–1976 Cultural Revolution, intense competition to be more revolutionary than the next person forced people to try to outdo each other in self-sacrifice and suffering. There were enormous political risks involved in any hint of "bourgeois" consumption; a person could be accused of bourgeois liberalism for growing a flower on a balcony, owning a cat or dog, or sitting on a padded chair. Meanwhile, Mao's campaigns to conquer nature felled forests to fuel makeshift steel furnaces, left forests denuded, and filled lakes and wetlands for ill-advised "Grain First" campaigns. Rivers were choked with the effluent of thousands of improperly sited and outfitted factories which had been relocated to the mountainous interior in the belief that they would be safer from aerial attack from the Russians. Urban "educated youth" were sent to China's border areas to prepare for war with the Soviet Union and Vietnam while remolding nature and themselves, even as professors and scholars who best understood the ecological value of biodiverse forests and wetlands were attacked as counter-revolutionaries and revisionists (Shapiro 2001). By the time of Mao's death in September 1976, China was isolated from much of the world, economically stagnant, and reeling from waves of political campaigns that had swept away the country's brightest, leaving survivors groping for ethical moorings.

The Chinese people then began to emerge from their long political and ideological nightmare. In December 1978, with the legendary Third Plenary Session of the 11th Chinese Communist Party Central Committee, reform-minded leaders such as Deng Xiaoping and Zhao Ziyang returned to power and endorsed a development program called the Four Modernizations (in agriculture, industry, defense, and science and technology), which opened China to the outside world after decades of isolation. Many of the new leaders had been victims of the Cultural Revolution. When they were sent to the countryside in punishment for their "counter-revolutionary" ideas, they saw firsthand how profoundly Mao's policies had failed the farmers. They launched a daring series of economic experiments to unleash the Chinese people's entrepreneurial initiative and to encourage their aspirations for better lives. Reforms spread gradually from rural areas to cities, where enterprises were made "responsible for their own profits and losses" rather than enjoying a guaranteed "iron rice bowl" of state support. With time, these reforms provided tremendous economic freedom, even to the point that China now seems more freewheelingly capitalistic than the West. Yet political reforms were limited, and village level elections were mostly prearranged until recent years. The Communist Party set policy, the national (State) government implemented it, and ordinary people had little ability to choose their leaders or their political system.

The Chinese people's desire for a better life after so much suffering, undergirded by their endless hard work and creativity, launched one of the greatest social transformations in history. A backlog of pent-up yearning for such basic creature comforts as upholstered furniture, wristwatches, bicycles, washing machines, and radios was gradually supplanted by a desire for status symbols and luxury goods. Rising expectations, intense competition, materialism, consumerism, and a focus on individual advancement replaced Mao-era slogans like "Serve the People" [*wei renmin fuwu* 为人民服务], which no longer carried weight. The Mao years left a legacy of corruption and disillusionment with the government which Chinese scholars and intellectuals have called a "crisis of confidence" [*xinyang weiji* 信仰危机] in public goals and values. The vacuum led people to cling to consumerism as a way to provide meaning to their lives and to be willing to tolerate a government which otherwise had betrayed them. There is much cynicism about public service or willingness to help anyone outside of personal networks, as seen during an October 2011 incident in Foshan in Guangdong Province, when passers-by failed to help a toddler who was struck by a vehicle, who was then, when no one stopped to help her, struck again and killed (Osnos 2014). Public outrage and widespread discussion of the lack of compassion in Chinese national character followed in microblogs and Internet polls. Activist Dai Qing told the *New York Times'* Michael Wines (2011) that the by-passers' callousness reflected a vacuum of beliefs: "All the traditional values of Chinese society were thrown out the window to make way for Mao and the rest of the party leadership. But that died long ago, and there was nothing to replace it except a materialistic hunger."

Whether environmental protection can ever become a shared public value under these circumstances is unclear (Bauer 2006). As far as environmental issues are concerned, there is an entrenched assumption, which is perhaps a legacy of the days when the government controlled all aspects of life, that even such public-spirited activities as cleaning trash from a river or from an apartment stairwell should be the job of the authorities. This attitude exacerbates tendencies to flout the law with respect to natural resources and/or pollution if so doing benefits oneself, one's family, and one's network of associates. (The melamine problem mentioned in previous chapters is a good example of this.) It also explains a tendency to litter, which reached a peak in the 1990s; Wang Yongchen, a journalist and founder of Green Earth Volunteers, began her career filing stories about the massive amounts of garbage left by Chinese tourists visiting Lake Dianchi near Kunming.

Mistrust of Party and government leadership, and concomitant lack of respect for regulations and common goals, have if anything been intensified by a traditional culture that emphasizes personal relationships, obligations, and connections rather than the rule of law. The post-Mao period has seen much waste of public assets and a culture of self-centeredness and desperation to succeed by any means. Frequent propaganda campaigns, and even executions of high-level officials for embezzlement and corruption, are aimed at stopping high officials' use of public funds for banquets, private cars, and brand name status symbols, but they seem to do little to change a national behavior pattern of wealth flaunting, self-interestedness, and disrespect for the law. Counterfeit currency, online scams, and fraudulent schemes abound at all levels of society. Moreover, the love of status symbols has fueled a huge market in fakes, creating a major international intellectual property headache and a cat-and-mouse effort to catch shipments of knockoff Gucci, Louis Vuitton, Burberry, Coach, and North Face products at customs checkpoints. Meanwhile, in the impoverished interior and rural backwaters near wealthy areas, the desperately poor dream of taking their turn. Young people often join "floating populations" in the slums of the big cities and sweatshops in manufacturing hubs in the Southeast, leaving their hometowns all but empty of laborers. The massive influx of migrant workers returning home for Spring Festival is an annual ritual that cripples the public transportation system.

A wonderful anecdote reported by Rebecca Marston of the BBC captures the focus on status of China's newly rich, as well as their emphasis on creating bonds of social obligation through generous gift-giving and sharing (2011). A group of wealthy businessmen were asked to bring their best bottles of imported wine to a gathering; some bottles cost as much as $1,600 apiece. They then poured them into a huge silver punchbowl and shared the contents as if they were so much sangria. (Other stories that also cause oenophiles to have heart attacks describe fine wines mixed with orange soda or Coke.) This story captures the emphasis on face and wealth display, on collective life and the forging of the bonds of *guanxi* [关系, or mutually indebted personal connections], and on the brash crudeness of some of China's nouveaux riches. The Chinese love of status symbols has been a godsend for Louis Vuitton, which already makes 40 percent of its profit from Chinese buyers, for Gucci, with more than 40 stores in China, and for Burberry, Rolls Royce, Audi and other pricey brands. China is number two in world consumption of luxury goods after Japan and ahead of the U.S. The Chinese are still trying to figure things out, however: I was once accosted by a young woman on the street in Chongqing wanting to know if "Malika" was a high status brand of cosmetics because she had just signed on to be a saleswoman. I eventually figured out she was talking about Mary Kay. In 2014, China remained the top buyer of luxury goods, with Chinese consumers purchasing 46% of global share (Xinhua 2015).

The Chinese focus on status symbols may sometimes seem puzzling, but the recent history of war, hardship, and political upheaval explains some of the intensity of the huge unmet consumer demand. An awareness of the Chinese people's tribulations of the last century may provide a sympathetic context for current high levels of conspicuous consumption (Yu 2014). However, it is sobering to consider the sharpening inequalities between rich and poor, coast and hinterland, for despite the high living standards of the middle and upper classes, millions of Chinese have yet to begin to satisfy their craving for consumption and wealth. According to the English-language official newspaper *China Daily*, the wealth gap between urban and rural Chinese is generally about 3.3 to 1, which Song Xiaowu, president of the China Society for Economic Reform, called an "appalling income disparity between the haves and have-nots" (Fu 2010). The sharp contrasts between rich and poor exacerbate the feeling of desperation among the poor and may contribute to the "me first" atmosphere that governs so many interactions. Migrant workers are motivated by "face" to send expensive gifts to their parents in the countryside and hide from them the harsh working conditions many of them endure in factories far from home, and are quick to seize on opportunities that appear to deliver a quick way out of poverty. So, too, are illegal immigrants in the West willing to endure tremendous privation and cruel working conditions. They must repay their "snakehead" smugglers and perform the Confucian duty of filial piety by sending home remittances and give their parents the "face" that comes with having offspring overseas.

As we see from the account above, China is engaged in a quest to reassert its historic great-power status, transforming urban landscapes, "conquering" nature with mega-projects, and engaging beyond its borders in ways designed to inspire notice and respect. Yet in the nationwide push for modernization, sustainability and social justice often fall by the wayside. During the past 30-plus years, China's economic growth and participation in global affairs have created some of the most dramatic social and economic changes ever to occur in a single country in such a short time; the prize of global respect is within reach. However, among the costs of such growth is some of the world's worst pollution, which threatens the people's health and well-being as well as the country's image in the world and the government's legitimacy at home. The most dramatic example of China's drive to achieve a modernity designed to inspire the world's respect is undoubtedly the Three Gorges Dam.

The Three Gorges Dam has traditional roots in the longing for relief from natural disasters, an extension of the responsibility imperial leaders felt to tame the rivers that have so often brought the Chinese people sorrow. Indeed, the dam can be understood as a triumph of the national longing for flood control, although when it was approved many of the arguments centered on energy production. The dam was a dream of modern China's founding father Sun Yat-sen in the early

20th century, and celebrated further by Mao in this well-known anonymous translation of his famous poem:

> Great plans are afoot:
> A bridge will fly to span the north and south,
> Turning a deep chasm into a thoroughfare;
> Walls of stone will stand upstream to the West
> To hold back Wushan's clouds and rain
> Until a smooth lake rises in the narrow gorges.
> The mountain goddess, if she is still there
> Will marvel at a world so changed.

Only after Mao's death, however, did technocratic leaders – led by the widely disliked former engineer and then-Premier Li Peng – have the technical and financial confidence to go forward with the plan. When the dam was approved, opposition in the National People's Congress and among ordinary people was widespread. Resistance was especially fierce in the region above the dam, among the citizens and intellectuals of the huge industrial city of Chongqing, which stood to see its Mao-era factories with their residues of toxic heavy metals inundated and the swiftly flowing Yangzi turned into a stagnant catch-all for garbage and sewage. However, opposition could be expressed only passively: A 1992 vote taken by the Congress saw most people withhold the usual rubber-stamp for Party decisions by refraining from raising their hands. The prominent anti-dam activist, NPC member and former nuclear physicist and engineer Dai Qing, edited two informative collections of essays about the risks of the dam, *Yangtze!,Yangtze!* (1994) and *The River Dragon Has Come: The Three Gorges Dam and the Fate of China's Yangtse River and Its People* (1998), and was later imprisoned for a year, nominally for her support of the 1989 Tiananmen protests. Today, the dam stands as a monument to man's hubris and China's desire to obtain the admiration of the world.

As predicted, it forcibly relocated more than two million people, was plagued with corruption and substandard construction and erosion, submerged rare archaeological structures, and likely dealt the last blow to the Yangzi River dolphin. Given their willingness to permit recent problems with the dam to be publicized, it is unlikely that the current group of Chinese leaders would have approved its current configuration, despite an official position that defends its flood control and electricity generation capacities. Nonetheless, small and large dams remain a critical part of China's plans to increase renewable energy percentages, despite frequent outcries about inadequate environmental impact assessments and siting on earthquake-prone grounds in the Far West, where much of China's unexploited hydropower potential lies. That a destructive project like the Three Gorges could be rammed through despite such widespread opposition gives little comfort to those concerned about some of the ambitious engineering efforts on the table today.

With little doubt, the modernization ethos, guided by the technocratic engineers who populate so many of the top echelons of China's Communist Party and state government, dominates and supersedes the traditions of Confucian sustainability, Buddhist reverence for life, and Daoist ecology. However, China's environmental problems do not lend themselves to a technological fix; they are political problems, social problems, and even problems of deep culture and philosophy. China's intellectuals understand the centrality of the culture question, and indeed they have been wrestling with it for more than 100 years.

DEBATE ABOUT CHINESE CULTURE

An old conundrum for educated Chinese is whether Chinese culture is stagnant, stifling, and feudalistic or the basis of a unique, harmonious, advanced, and superior Eastern civilization (Link 1992). During the late Qing dynasty at the turn of the 20th century, there was a protracted public debate about whether aspects of foreign culture could be used selectively to serve China – could China simply adopt the West's technology or must it also import Western ideas? During the 1919 May Fourth movement, a time of democratic expression and intellectual ferment, young people consciously rejected Chinese feudalistic and paternalistic social structures and embraced modern Western literature, lifestyles, and political ideas. In the early 1920s, the novella, *The True Story of Ah Q*, a masterpiece by Lu Xun, portrayed the Chinese people as rationalizing their oppression and humiliation with infantilism, passivity, and self-deception. Much more recently, in 1988, the documentary film maker Su Xiaokang took up some of the same themes in his six-part series, "River Elegy" [*heshang* 河殇]. By portraying the traditional symbol of Chinese greatness, the Great Wall, as a source of conservatism and isolation and contrasting the invigorating "blue" seas of modern foreign ideas with the dried-up culture of the Yellow River (widely known as the cradle of Chinese civilization), he captured Chinese intellectuals' deep ambivalence about Chinese tradition, so often experienced as stultifying and insular, as compared with fresh ideas from the outside world. The political sensitivity of this critique of traditional Chinese culture, which preceded the 1989 Tiananmen demonstrations which were the greatest threat to the power of the Chinese Communist Party since their victory in 1949, resulted in the filmmaker being driven into exile in the U.S. In China, the nationwide criticism and denunciation of the film blamed it for promoting bourgeois ideas and contributing to student unrest.

The ongoing vitality and urgency of the debate over national identity is reflected in the enormous popularity of Jiang Rong's 2008 semiautobiographical novel, *Wolf Totem* (published in 2004 as *Lang Tuteng* 狼图腾 in Chinese), which sold so many copies in China that only the little red book, *Quotations from Chairman Mao*, has sold more. The lead character is a Han Chinese "sent down" to Inner Mongolia in the 1960s, where he learns the secrets of indigenous knowledge about the relationship between wolves and the grasslands ecosystem and then witnesses how Han culture destroys that balance. Settlers eradicate the wolves that keep the gazelles in check. They destroy the grasslands and the creatures that live on it by turning them into farmland. Weak and passive Han culture is contrasted with the wild courage of the Mongol herdsmen (connected to that of the wolf), and thus the novel becomes an indictment of Han Chinese passivity as compared with the courage of the meat-eating, wolf-like natives. It is an elegy for the ethnic minority culture, grasslands, and the creatures destroyed wantonly by Han bureaucrats and settlers.

Nowadays, variations of the same debate continue as a quiet struggle rages over China's national identity. There are unresolved questions about the legacy of the Mao period, doubts about the legitimacy of the Chinese Communist Party, and competing visions of the country's guiding values and goals. Most of this discussion takes place at the margins of social, political, and intellectual life, expressed indirectly in the press and academic studies because a full airing of the issues might call the government's legitimacy into question. Yet its implications for China's development are enormous. The value placed on "face" sometimes leads a country to make ill-considered judgments about the use of national funds, as occurred when so much money was spent on the Three Gorges Dam and is now being spent on space exploration, when China would be better served by investing in improving the lot of the poor. But there is hope that the narrative of sustainability may yet become strong enough to guide China's development decisions. Acknowledging the spirit of national questioning, the central government has attempted to shape the conversation by introducing the notion of a "China Dream." This is meant to spur ordinary people to help realize a collective Chinese vision of well-being, with the implication that this is quite different from the "American dream" of individual freedom and material consumption. Although so far the China Dream seems to emphasize prosperity and national rejuvenation, sustainability has also been a theme in the conversation.

China's people face a long list of questions about their identity; both the government and the newly ambitious citizenry have some soul-searching to do. Is China to look to the past and reconnect with its heritage of civility, respect for the ancient and pragmatic understanding of the value of sustainable management practices? Is China to focus on the present moment as it builds wealth and power and expends its energies on material success? Is China to look toward the future to become an innovator in the search for new models of sustainable development and a leader in global citizenship? How are the Chinese people to understand their history and destiny, with memories of past humiliations so vivid, and nagging suspicions that flaws in national culture and character may have contributed to the country's suffering and may yet presage future disasters? How is China's government to deal with the painful legacy of the Cultural Revolution and the Tiananmen massacre, and with the enormous pressures of exploding consumption demands and mounting environmental problems? These questions recur as the Chinese struggle to find guidance through the environmental quagmire: Does the answer lie in the Confucian tradition of harmony between the heavens – often understood as nature – and man [*tian-ren heyi* 天人合一] as a way of building social stability? Is it in the Buddhist tradition of reverence for life? Or perhaps in the Daoist "Way" of accommodating nature and going with the flow? Or, as contemporary policy makers seem to believe, in a blend of Maoist and capitalist modernization and nature conquest? Is the solution to "return to the roots" as seen in the fashion for things Tibetan and rural, or to turn outwards to the West and adopt the ethos of the global environmental movement? Do Chinese ideas of nature provide the most guidance, or those of foreign environmentalists? Does the answer lie with the individual or the collective? Discussions of many of these questions are nascent, but the government's fear of organized groups and its desire to control the official version of China's recent history, particularly the Cultural Revolution, acts as a deterrent to a full and open national dialogue.

As we have seen in this chapter, the Chinese people seem at times to swing between jingoism, or pugnacious nationalism, and insecurity, or what a psychologist might call "low self-esteem." Every interaction with outsiders is the more sensitive because it is scrutinized for evidence of China's relative status. Traditions that emphasize social hierarchy, which are also very much alive in other Confucian societies like Taiwan, Japan, and Singapore, have become exaggerated as China flexes its muscles in international politics. The deep-rooted concern for "face" has colored China's development decisions, leading the government to put resources into tangible, image-building achievements, coupled with efforts to reach out internally and internationally to guarantee supplies of energy, grain, and raw materials and to "pacify the borders" once and for all. Often, such decisions are detrimental to social needs. We have also seen how traditional beliefs can have an impact on endangered species and biodiversity all around the world. Despite this historical cultural baggage, however, there are signs that an alternative model of development is also emerging. There is more discussion of sustainable development at the top levels of Chinese leadership than in almost any Western country, and incentives for industry to create "green" jobs and innovations are significant. The stalled effort to establish an annual "Green GDP" to evaluate the environmental costs of economic development may be revived. The stringent automobile fuel efficiency standards are a credit to the nation. Reconsideration of and debate over plans to build multiple dams on the pristine Nu River and Upper Yangzi in Yunnan may reduce their number and degree of impact. There is thus a possibility that China's preoccupation with "face" and national identity may yet be channeled in support of an alternative model that the world has not yet seen. Of course, there is no simple, direct causal relationship between attitudes and beliefs, on the one hand, and behavior and policy on the other (Bruun and Kalland 1995); a solid environmental education for all children and public promotion of "green" values would not be sufficient to shift China or the world onto a less damaging path. However, they may be necessary first steps. China may be able to resolve its environmental crisis using technological leapfrogging and courageous policy making to become a global leader in truly sustainable development. For this transformation to succeed, however, a national dialogue and effort to promote a "green" national identity, and to engage and empower public participation and civil society, will be required.

QUESTIONS FOR RESEARCH AND DISCUSSION

1 To what extent do you think that traditional Chinese attitudes and beliefs shape behavior and policy with respect to interaction with the non-human world? Are teaching values of sustainability and strong scientific training about the costs of global resource depletion and pollution necessary to shift human interactions with non-human nature in China? Is a spiritual renaissance the answer? Is your response the same or different for your own country?

2 How does China's history affect its citizens' attitudes toward China's role in the world? How might that history affect China's prospects for sustainable development? Can you discuss this question for your own country?

3 How do culinary, medical, and philosophical traditions affect relationships with non-human species in China? In your country?

4 Given the Chinese people's recent history of privation, should we feel surprised at the new culture of conspicuous consumption? How important is material wealth to living a good life?

5 In what ways does the Chinese relationship with the environment mirror that of all humans living on the planet? Can you find any resemblances between the Han Chinese modern relationship with nature and that of global modern society, and what are the differences? Do you feel that the prospects for China to address its environmental concerns are better than those for the globe as a whole, worse, or the same?

6 How is Chinese national identity different from yours? How is it similar? Can you identify an environmental issue where you could find common ground with Chinese attitudes? Is there any evidence in your country of a sustainability ethic? If so, what are its core elements?

ADDITIONAL RESOURCES

- Forum on Religion and Ecology (Yale University), at: http://bioethics.yale.edu/resources/forum-religion-and-ecology
- Gary Marcuse, "Searching for Sacred Mountain" (Film), available at: http://pulitzercenter.org/reporting/searching-sacred-mountain-religion-environment-gary-marcuse-shi-lihong
- Orville Schell, "China: Humiliation and the Olympics," July 2008. Available on the *New York Review of Books* website.
- TRAFFIC information on TCM and the trade in endangered species: www.traffic.org
- Lu Xun, *The True Story of Ah Q* (1921), Marxists Internet Archive, at: http://www.marxists.org/archive/lu-xun/1921/12/ah-q/index.htm

5 | Public Participation and Civil Society: The View from Below

Chinese civil society faces severe limitations in its ability to organize, communicate, and conduct activities. Yet even as there are tremendous changes with respect to the environment from the top down, as well as new demands for pollution controls and food safety from influential middle-class consumers, the grass roots are feeling their power and becoming active. They often form partnerships with the upper reaches of the bureaucracy in order to pressure corrupt developers, self-interested local officials, lower- and middle-level bureaucrats and polluting factory operators. Almost all citizens' groups cultivate ties with top leaders and agencies as a form of protection and assurance of a green light for their activities.

It is important not to over-generalize about Chinese civil society, for China is a large, diverse, and unevenly developed country, with unequal distribution of resources and local empowerment. The eastern seaboard and urban areas have different characteristics and dynamics than rural areas and interior western provinces. Nonetheless, even in remote areas such as the Nu River region near Myanmar and the Upper Yangzi near the Tibetan Autonomous Region, there are signs of an increasingly vibrant civil society. Indeed, environmental organizing in Yunnan province in the Southwest is in some ways more free than in Beijing. Moreover, as we will see in the next chapter, some less developed regions of Western China are hothouses of biodiversity inhabited by ethnic minority nationality people, who often have political reasons for resisting the dominance of the Han. This combination contributes to environmental activism in remote areas where it might not be expected and draws the attention of urban elites intent on intervening in dam projects and resource extractions that degrade landscapes and threaten biodiversity. However, because of the politically sensitive combination of minority populations and resources problems, the government often construes such environmental activism as ethnic unrest. Minorities are thus at a double disadvantage when polluting or extractive industries arrive in their regions.

Not all Chinese public participation is expressed through citizens' groups. Complaint hotlines provide government-organized safety valves for individuals to register discontent with polluting factories (Brettell 2008). Moreover, "environmental mass incidents," as the government calls such protests, are astonishingly numerous. In some cases, public participation is fueled by localized pollution and arises spontaneously through cell-phone messaging and social media such as *weibo*, the Chinese version of Twitter. In other cases, NGO activists lead the way to greater citizen participation by conducting information sessions and providing advice and legal support.

Despite such new opportunities, there is continued repression of environmental activists and ordinary citizens who face monitoring, detention, or imprisonment because of their protests. Information may be censored, activist groups are watched, and there can be heavy penalties for unsanctioned public assembly. Even top environmental officials' candid statements about China's dire environmental conditions and the need for more transparency of information about pollution may carry political risks.

This chapter presents a snapshot of China's emerging environmental civil society. We explore the regulatory and financial framework in which such organizations exist. We discuss the challenge for civil society groups seeking to influence public behavior and power, especially under China's authoritarian conditions – Chinese ENGOs have built on the standard tactics of international ENGOs in spectacularly creative ways in order to craft a more sustainable way forward. Then we illustrate these tactics through a series of more-or-less chronological examples, from the first effort to save the Tibetan Antelope through cutting-edge efforts to use class-action lawsuits to hold polluters accountable. These examples will allow us to "meet" some of China's environmental heroes and key organizations. Next we discuss citizen activists, who are thrust into political roles when their communities face powerful environmental challenges. We conclude with a short discussion of the role of foreign ENGOs and government-organized NGOs (GONGOs) and think tanks.

OPERATING FRAMEWORK

In China, citizens' groups (non-governmental organizations) are classic illustrations of the Gramscian argument that civil society is often penetrated by the state as a way of manipulating culture so as to gain consent for government rule. The Communist Party issued regulations regarding the registration of social groups as a priority immediately after the 1949 Maoist revolution, when the Chinese government viewed independent social organizations as potential threats to the governance of the Communist Party. Under the 1950 registration measures, most social organizations were suppressed as feudal or reactionary organizations, while the few that survived were subsumed into the government system or transformed into government affiliates.

During the Mao years, particularly during the 1966–76 Cultural Revolution, independent social organizations simply could not exist: Aside from Communist mass organizations such as the Young Pioneers, Communist Youth Leagues, and neighborhood associations that were effectively decentralized monitoring networks to allow the Party to keep tabs on citizens, other social groups were treated as counter-revolutionary and their leaders persecuted. Although the ultra-leftist, often fascist Red Guard organizations arguably had their own aspects of public participation and democratic expression, the period was marked by extreme violence toward religious groups, artists and writers, educated people of all persuasions, and anyone with foreign ties. Dictatorship, anarchy, chaos, and economic stagnation marked the decade.

After Mao died and Deng Xiaoping came into power with his economic reforms and modernization platform, more space became available for individual expression, freedom of information, and participation in unofficial social groups. From 1979 to 1989, the number of national-level social organizations increased 16-fold, reaching an official figure of 1,600. Recent Civil Affairs Bureau figures show officially registered groups numbering as many as 500,000. A social organization must be authorized by a government agency in order to be legally registered; some social groups have nicknamed their supervisor their "mother-in-law." The supervising agency is responsible for the group's ideology, finance and personnel, research, contacts with foreign organizations, and donations from overseas (Teets 2014). Registration is very difficult because most governmental agencies are hesitant to take responsibility for the behavior of a citizens' group. Having a supervisory body also undermines a group's independence, so some organizations register as business entities, while many more operate underground without legal identities, such as the illegal pro-Vatican Catholic Church and various human rights and democracy groups. By some estimates, almost 90 percent of China's social groups are unregistered and cannot have a bank account under the organization's name or enjoy other perquisites like tax breaks. This lack of financial recognition complicates their ability to receive donations and makes their activities expensive.

Despite these difficulties, NGO registration policy seems to be easing in some cities in recent years, especially for pilot projects. In 2008, Shenzhen opened up registration for social organizations in the fields of social welfare and charity, and in July 2011, Minister of Civil

circumvent government filters and censorship, as when the phrases "taking a walk" and "going sightseeing " were used in several cities to coordinate public protests, and when in 2008 citizens of Shanghai opposed the building of a magnetic levitation rail line through their neighborhood and organized themselves to "take a walk" on certain days. The phrase is so innocuous and the words in it so common that it cannot be filtered and banned, and participants cannot be arrested because they can claim that they just happened to be in the area. One of the better-known Weibo posts was a February 2013 message by Zhejiang eyeglasses entrepreneur Jin Zengmin, whose sister died at an early age of cancer. Jin offered 200,000 renminbi to a top local environmental official if he would swim in the shoe factory-polluted waters of Rui'an, near Shanghai, for 20 minutes. The official refused and the challenge went viral, becoming a powerful example of the Internet's potential as a tool to pressure local agencies to do their jobs.

Online petitioning has also become a critical form of social mobilization. Internet petitions to clean up Beijing's air have included demands for greater information transparency and the distribution of free face masks. In an international echo of the tradition of appealing to powerful figures, in May 2013 a Chengdu resident opposing an oil refinery posted a petition on the U.S. White House website. The petition received several thousand signatures, and the police visited the petitioner to demand that she take it down, which she could not do.

Many ordinary Chinese have motivations for environmental activism thrust upon them when their villages are contaminated by factories and strange cancer clusters appear, or when a lake that they rely upon for fishing becomes toxic. Even fairly uneducated peasant-farmers can become activists in such situations, especially if the pollution or dam gains the attention of an NGO or journalist. One such example is that of the farmer profiled in a remarkable documentary, "Warriors of Qiugang" (Yang 2010). Educated environmental activists provided support to this local leader in his efforts to get a pesticide and dye factory to close down and clean up, but the risk and determination was his alone. Despite the fact that the private owners of the factory had strong ties to local leaders, villagers fought desperately through petitions, lawsuits, and demonstrations, and eventually succeeded in getting the factory to shut. As of the end of the film, however, villagers continued to die of cancer and the toxic waste remained.

This sort of peasant-farmer activism is less likely to succeed than efforts of more educated middle-class citizens. In the Northern city of Dalian in August 2011, for example, citizens protested against the Fujia paraxylene (PX) plant, whose dyke was breached by high ocean waves during a typhoon. As readers will remember, PX is a toxic petrochemical used in the fabric industry to make polyester and other synthetics, and the citizens of Xiamen on the Southern coast successfully fought a similar PX plant in 2007, when citizens mobilized themselves via cell phone messages to rally against a plant planned by the Xianglu Tenglong Group. The 2011 protests in Dalian seem to have met with the most rapid government response so far. Such protests can be understood as a wave of "not in my back yard-ism" (NIMBYism) on the part of a newly empowered Chinese middle class. Unfortunately, in most cases, as elsewhere in the world, NIMBYism often results in the removal of the offending project to a more vulnerable, less well organized community, as we will see in the next chapter.

Dalian citizens, learning from their Xiamen neighbors, also used cell texting to organize protests against the plant. According to one news story, "Protesters including children marched holding banners that declared: 'I love Dalian and reject poison,' 'Return me my home and garden, get out PX, protect Dalian,' and 'Return my future generations' beautiful home'" (Wee 2011). The authorities, too, seem to have learned from the Xiamen example. The Communist Party chief and the mayor quickly promised to shut and relocate the plant. Protesters were not satisfied without a firm timetable, and their anger broadened against government corruption in general: The plant had been in operation several years before the requisite environmental impact assessment was conducted and approved. In the face of organized, educated, urban middle-class mobilization, the government backed down. Greenpeace's China program director Ma Tianjie told *The Hindu,* "We are seeing more and more cases of middle-class urban residents saying no to polluting projects, and getting involved in such issues . . . In urban areas, people are increasingly more aware. With online tools like microblogs, it is also becoming easier to communicate issues to the public" (Krishnan 2011). Indeed, these protests seem to be increasing as the middle class in other cities learns of the success of such protests. Soon after the Dalian incident, protesters in a city near Shanghai demonstrated against a chronically polluting solar panel production plant, while in December 2011, protesters in the fishing village of Haimen in Guangdong province blocked an expressway in opposition to a planned coal-fired power plant, claiming that existing plants had caused cancer and a drop in fishing yields. This protest ended in violent confrontations with riot police and a suspension of the project. Protests over similar issues have followed regularly. Calls for government transparency and accountability are thus increasingly accompanying the thousands of "environmental mass incidents." Exact figures are difficult to determine, with many reports mentioning 80,000–100,000 mass incidents per year, not all of them about the environment. That the government reports such incidents in the official press is encouraging, perhaps indicative of increased confidence in addressing public outrage.

There are many other cases of local citizens trying to hold polluting enterprises accountable, but their stories are largely left untold to the outside world. Consider the parents of children with lead poisoning, or the residents of Panyu, Guangdong Province, whose citizen lawsuit eventually forced the Dongtai tannery to pay compensation after discharging contaminated wastewater. Also largely unknown to the international community is the story of local Huai River defender Huo Daishan, who was motivated to do something about the extensive chemical effluents in the river when his childhood friend died of cancer, or the effort in Hunan province's Xiangtan city, where an ordinary citizen's online "green appeal" petition to clean up Yujia Lake successfully pressured officials to promise to reverse pollution trends.

Often this kind of activism is met with threats and political repression, as these "ordinary people" do not usually have the backing of international ties or sophistication in navigating the political system, unlike highly educated urban activists. They are fighting powerful developers, factory owners, and political interests. Many farmers faced with dislocation for dams simply acknowledge their own powerlessness in the face of the state. They know the risks in resisting and believe it to be dangerous, if not futile. They fear the experience of Lake Tai activist Wu Lihong who, after tirelessly fighting to clean one of China's largest and most polluted bodies of water, was sentenced to prison in 2007 on a trumped-up charge of extortion and blackmail. Zhejiang activist and founder of "Green Watch" Tan Kai was arrested for illegally obtaining "state secrets" in 2005 and denied legal representation. He served a full 18-month sentence. An activist working to clean up Dianchi Lake in Yunnan Province was threatened and beaten. In addition, farmers resisting forcible relocations for the Three Gorges Dam have been arrested and prosecuted. Meanwhile, as mentioned, nature reserve officers have died fighting poachers, like the previously mentioned Tibetan brothers-in-law who died defending the Tibetan antelope.

In sum, the tools and techniques available to Chinese ENGOs and ordinary citizens have evolved dramatically since the mid-1990s, creating a sort of "environmental activism with Chinese characteristics," in which tacit alliances with sympathetic government officials and agencies allow Chinese civil society to operate in a political space where boundaries are not completely clear, but have been steadily expanding in exciting new ways. However, the best efforts of Chinese citizens to speak out against pollution and to curb the corrupt practices that have so profoundly destroyed the environment have thus far yielded only limited success. Sam Geall's excellent edited volume of case studies, *China and the Environment: The Green Revolution* (2013) provides greater detail about some of the campaigns mentioned above, and about the immense challenges that Chinese ENGOs and ordinary citizens are facing.

GOVERNMENT-ORGANIZED NGOS (GONGOS)

In addition to ENGOs founded by intellectuals, students, and grass-roots environmental activists, ENGOs established by governmental agencies and governmental officials also play an important role in international environmental cooperation, environmental education, and environmental campaigns. These groups can play a very positive role for the environment, for in reality Chinese political life takes its cues from the central government and the central government is far from monolithic. Such GONGOs are often strong voices for environmental protection from within the government (Wu, Fengshi 2002). Among top-down organized and funded GONGOs, one of the largest is the above-mentioned All-China Environment Federation (ACEF), founded in 2005 under the patronage of the State Environmental Protection Administration (now Ministry of Environmental Protection). Its website describes it as a non-profit national social organization, but we can easily see the close governmental ties in its mandate:

The Federation aims to implement the strategy of sustainable development, achieve the goal of environment and development as set out by the State, and to safeguard the environmental interests of the public and the society. The major tasks are to keep contacts with influential and high-profile senior personages, unite a variety of social groups, and play the role of solidarity and coherence; put forward proposals on government environmental decision-making; provide services on environmental laws for the public and the society; enable the public and the society to get access to environmental information, and conduct activities for environmental publicity and education; promote the sound development of China's environmental NGOs and help them build and obtain their due position in international communities; and undertake other work as entrusted by the government and relevant organizations.

Another prominent GONGO is the China Environmental Protection Foundation (CEPF) established by Qu Geping, the first Administrator of SEPA, whose book on China's population we have already mentioned. The organization can be traced to the seminal 1992 U.N. Conference on Environment and Development in Rio de Janeiro, Brazil, where Qu Geping shared the $100,000 UNEP Sasakawa Prize for his contributions to environmental protection. In accepting the award, he announced he would use it to establish a fund for environmental work in China. One year later, with support from SEPA and other central governmental agencies, the CEPF was raising funds for environmental protection, facilitating environmental cooperation between China and other countries, and issuing grants for environmental projects. Most board members of the CEPF have governmental backgrounds and, like the All-China Environment Federation, the CEPF's supervisory body is the Ministry of Environmental Protection. It has awarded the China Environment Prize to individuals and organizations that have made prominent contributions to environmental protection since 2000, and funded numerous environmental projects, such as the Ecology Great Wall project, which supports tree planting and sustainable agricultural programs in rural northwest China.

Some university think tanks, like Ma Zhong's Beijing Environment and Development Institute at Renmin University, also occupy middle grounds between state-run institutions with considerable leeway and truly independent citizens' groups. However, although the number of

GONGOs is far more numerous than those mentioned here, there are fewer than that of the bottom-up organizations, and the Ministry of Environmental Protection and local environmental bureaus have begun to cooperate directly with grassroots ENGOs.

ROLE OF INTERNATIONAL ENGOS

International NGOs have been eager to work in China but have faced numerous difficulties getting visas and permits and finding Chinese partners, a basic requirement to be able to operate inside the country. Tsinghua University has estimated that as many as 10,000 international NGOs are active in China, not only on environmental issues but also on poverty reduction, governance, journalist training, and other public concerns. One of the best respected of these, China Development Brief, is an informational and networking project for foreign development, charitable, and environmental groups. Founded in 1996, it was shut down in 2007 after more than a decade of dedicated work when the government created visa problems for English director Nick Young. He was accused of conducting unauthorized surveys and was forced to leave the country. Still, an all-Chinese version of the organization survives. Some fear that the spring 2015 regulations requiring international NGOs to register with a Chinese government entity, forbidding them from raising money within the country, and otherwise restricting their activities in the country, are intended to curtail their influence and in some cases simply drive them out.

The large international conservation NGO World Wide Fund for Nature (WWF) was the first international ENGO to have a significant presence in China, and has worked in China's Western provinces of Yunnan and Sichuan for decades, adopting the giant panda as its international logo (Schaller 1993). Conservation International and the Nature Conservancy have more recently established strong programs, with the Nature Conservancy undertaking to develop and conserve some of China's most beautiful but endangered regions through its Yunnan Great Rivers project. Conservation International has seen its role primarily as a networker and facilitator, although it also develops conservation models and remains a strong player on the ground, educating consumers in big cities on how to reduce the consumption of wildlife products.

Many other international environmental groups also have an active presence in China. The Natural Resources Defense Council is working on climate change, green building and clean energy, environmental governance and green supply chains. Environmental Defense has pioneered carbon trading experiments using market-based approaches to conservation. The World Resources Institute works on population and health as well as transportation. The Sierra Club focuses on energy and trade issues. Pacific Environment focuses on transboundary problems in the Pacific Rim. The International Fund for Animal Welfare, which faces a tremendous task because of China's abominable practices of animal cruelty, is trying to pass animal welfare laws and create a shelter system. One of the early groups to make contact in China was the independent Friends of the Earth Hong Kong (Hong Kong has been part of China since 1997 but operates under a more democratic political system). Greenpeace, which is widely admired and respected in China, similarly based most of its work from Hong Kong, but its Beijing office and large in-country staff have now grown. The group has taken on such causes as e-waste, genetically modified organisms, toxics, and information transparency around air pollution. Such groups generally nurture strong alliances with the Ministry of Environmental Protection as a way of gaining assurance that they will be able to continue their work. While such alliances may limit them, they reflect the Chinese political reality that NGOs need support, whether from the state or from foreign donors. In fact, even the voices for environmental protection within the central government are not immune from political threat. By working together, civil society and the parts of the central administration trying to shift China onto a more sustainable path strive to strengthen each other and carve out additional political space.

In addition to the big international NGOs with a presence in China, there have been increased efforts by smaller issue-oriented NGOs and domestic groups to link with neighboring countries to tackle transboundary issues. International Rivers, based in Berkeley, California, has partnered with small NGOs in the lower reaches of the Salween River in Myanmar and Thailand, as well as China to work against the dams planned for the Nu River (as the Salween is called in China). Through blogging, public media campaigns, documentary films, and other modes of political engagement (primarily of the symbolic politics type), the group has helped Chinese grassroots groups coalesce around an issue which is both romantic, in that it appeals to young Chinese students' sense of adventure tourism and interest in the exoticism of ethnic minority areas, and hard-hitting, in that it goes to the core of China's energy policy. After fervent public opposition, in 2004 the Chinese government suspended plans for the dams pending further environmental review (Mertha 2008), but the 12th Five-Year Plan put some of the Nu River dams back on the table. Despite opposition, hydropower remains a centerpiece of China's renewable energy portfolio. The Japanese nuclear disaster caused the Chinese to be more cautious in their nuclear plans, especially in earthquake-prone regions, putting renewed pressure on rivers. Even the massive dam on the Upper Yangzi River at Tiger Leaping Gorge, cancelled after local protests, could yet be revived, or moved upriver toward Tibet.

This chapter has illustrated the connection between environmental protection and political repression in developing countries. In developed countries, activists often work in different spheres than do those concerned with human rights. However, in the developing world, this sharp distinction often does not exist, for two main reasons: First, the political rights of environmental activists to free speech and assembly, due process, and freedom from torture are often violated, so environmentalists can potentially become human rights victims themselves. Second, in the developing world, with its intense pollution problems, the right to clean air, water, and food is clearly identified with the right to life, the most fundamental of all the human rights. At the global level, an effort to articulate these connections has been ongoing in the form of the Earth Charter Initiative, where a multinational team of activists and civil society groups has drafted a document expressing the connections among ecological protection, justice, peace, democracy, and human rights. Although activists hope that it will someday formally be signed at the United Nations like the human rights covenants, to date the initiative has flourished primarily at the grass roots. The charter has been endorsed primarily by civil society groups, although international organizations such as the United Nations Educational, Scientific and Cultural Organization (UNESCO) and the International Union for Conservation of Nature (IUCN) have also supported it. The Initiative's official mission is "to promote the transition to sustainable ways of living and a global society founded on a shared ethical framework that includes respect and care for the community of life, ecological integrity, universal human rights, respect for diversity, economic justice, democracy, and a culture of peace." By articulating values in this way, the Earth Charter Initiative shows how civil society can participate in global governance without formal governmental approval or power.

QUESTIONS FOR RESEARCH AND DISCUSSION

1 Can you identify some of the creative ways that Chinese advocacy groups have attempted to achieve their goals? Can you suggest additional strategies they might employ? What are the strengths and limitations of Internet-based activism?

2 How does the situation of Chinese activists shed light on the relationship between environmental protection and human rights? Compare the Universal Declaration of Human Rights with the Earth Charter (both easily available online). Which would be easier to implement and enforce in China and in your own country? Where are the areas of overlap and divergence?

3 What is the role of China's middle class in environmental change? Is its newfound wealth a positive or negative force, or both? What is the connection between the rise of the middle class and civil society?

4 What do you think about the role of GONGOs in China? Are they an effective way for the government to mobilize people while exerting a measure of social control? Do different advocacy groups have different approaches to try to create social change? Where are the leverage points for social change in your community?

ADDITIONAL RESOURCES

- "Apple Opens Up: IT Industry Supply Chain Investigative Report, Phase VI," by Friends of Nature, Institute for the Public Environment, Envirofriends, Nature University, and Nanjing Greenstone. Available at: 114.215.104.68:89/Upload/Report-IT -Phase-VI-EN.pdf
- "Rainmakers," a documentary by Floris-Jan Van Luyn. Information available at: http://www.imdb.com/title/tt1688074/
- "Shielding the Mountains," a documentary by Emily Yeh. Information available at: http://www.tibetsacredmountain.org
- "Shifting Nature," part three of the PBS documentary "China from the Inside" by Jonathan Lewis. Information and trailer available at: http://www.pbs.org/kqed/chinainside/nature/index.html

- "Silent Nu River," a documentary by Hu Jie. Information and trailer available at: http://www.visiblerecord.com/en/films/?id=C010
- "Under the Dome," a documentary by Chai Jing. Available (with English subtitles) on Youtube.
- "Waking the Green Tiger," a documentary by Gary Marcuse. Information and trailer available at: www.facetofacemedia.ca/page.php?sectionID=2
- "Warriors of Qiugang," 39-minute documentary by Ruby Yang and Thomas Lennon. Full film available at: http://e360.yale.edu/feature/the_warriors_of_qiugang_a_chinese_village_fights_back/2358/
- U.S. Embassy-Beijing, list of Chinese environmental NGOs at: http://beijing.usembassy-china.org.cn/esth_engo.html
- Wolfgang Sachs, Environment and Human Rights, Wuppertal Paper No. 137 (September 2003), Wuppertal Institute for Climate, Environment, and Energy. Available at: http://www.uibk.ac.at/peacestudies/downloads/peacelibrary/environment.pdf

6 Environmental Justice and the Displacement of Environmental Harm

The inseparable links between environmental sustainability and social justice are increasingly well recognized. Without social justice, the extraction of resources all too often simply displaces harm across time and space, postponing our confrontation with the limits of the planet's bounty and concealing the costs of our consumption. Some would also extend the concern for justice across species, as humans encroach on the habitat of other living creatures and drive them to extinction, tearing apart the web of life on which we ultimately depend. This chapter focuses on achieving justice across geographic space in the human world. First, however, let us reflect on the temporal dimensions of this problem.

Great attention has been paid to the fact that the world is reaching the limits to resources – indeed, our basic understanding of sustainability rests on the effort to achieve equity between those now alive and those not yet born, or justice for future generations. Unfortunately, traditional economic systems, from Marxism to capitalism, have failed to account for the depletion of natural capital and have often measured environmental degradation or resources consumption as simply another form of economic activity contributing to growth. The inadequacy of these theories is clearly demonstrated in our study of the environmental crisis in China: Aggressive development without internalization of real environmental costs, left unchecked, could undermine many of China's gains. Minerals, fossil fuels, timber, and agricultural resources are growing scarce, even as China's heavy pollution, which is increasingly inflicted on the poor and vulnerable, damages public health. Social unrest over environmental problems threatens the government's credibility, authority, and legitimacy.

Increasingly, the world's policy makers are paying attention not only to the temporal dimensions of displacement of harm but also to the spatial ones. For those who are sensitive to the dynamic of displacement, sustainability will never be achieved without distributive justice among those currently alive. *Inter-generational equity*, which considers the rights of future generations to the same "natural capital" available to people alive today, cannot be separated from the politically contentious *intra-generational equity*, which considers the rights of all people to have fair access to and benefits from the world's resources. The United Nations Development Program (UNDP)'s 2011 annual report, *Sustainability and Equity: A Better Future for All* elaborates on the links between environmental degradation and injustice:

> A joint lens shows how environmental degradation intensifies inequality through adverse impacts on already disadvantaged people and how inequalities in human development amplify environmental degradation . . . Inequalities are especially unjust when they systematically disadvantage specific groups of people, whether because of gender, race or birthplace, or when the gap is so great that acute poverty is high. (Klugman 2011)

In another indication of the wide acceptance of these links, the United Nations environmental conferences, Stockholm (1972), Rio de Janeiro (1992), and Johannesburg (2002), affirmed that sustainability rests on three pillars – environmental, economic, and social – while the Earth Summit in Rio de Janeiro (2012) focused on creating an institutional framework for sustainable development in the context of poverty eradication. The Earth Charter, mentioned in the previous chapter, also plumbs these interconnections.

Environmental injustice across space occurs at many different levels and scales. It can occur within large cities among neighborhoods; between urban and rural areas; between wealthy and less wealthy regions within a single country; and across borders, between countries forced by economic necessity to receive environmental harms and those who can afford to export them. We have already noted the extreme wealth gap between residents of Chinese cities and those living in the countryside, and seen how poor communities, less well-organized and politically powerful than their neighbors, often bear the brunt when a well-organized urban middle class forces a polluting factory to relocate. This chapter explores these ideas in greater detail. We home in on several examples: First we look at the problems of where to site land-fills, at the unhealthy living conditions of the millions of rural migrants who make up the "floating populations" in the slums outside some of China's major cities, and at rural "cancer villages." The bulk of the chapter then explores regional inequalities between the wealthy coastal areas in the East and the less developed Western border regions, where so many ethnic minority nationalities live. Tensions in places like Tibet, Xinjiang, and Inner Mongolia are fraught with implications for China's future as a unified state capable of delivering justice and a good liveli-hood to all of its citizens. We finally turn to international examples. In some cases, China is an importer and victim of environmental injustice, as in Southern Guangzhou, a center for the international electronic waste recycling business. However, China is also an exporter and source of environmental injustice, as the newly wealthy country dis-places environmental harms onto less developed countries, extracting resources from Ecuador, Nigeria, and elsewhere, often creating pollu-tion and environmental degradation in the process. Although the latter topic is largely beyond the scope of a volume that focuses on domestic problems, it is much in the news these days as countries try to under-stand how China's rise will affect them, on the one hand welcoming Chinese aid and investment, and on the other wary about becoming dependent upon a new superpower whose role in the international system is still being defined.

We must start with a few definitions of the interrelated concepts of environmental justice and environmental injustice. The Central European University Center for Environmental Policy and Law (2007) provides these useful articulations:

> A condition of environmental justice exists when environmental risks and hazards and investments and benefits are equally distributed with a lack of discrimination, whether direct or indirect, at any jurisdictional level; and when access to environmental investments, benefits, and natural resources are equally distributed; and when access to information, participation in decision making, and access to justice in environment-related matters are enjoyed by all.

By contrast,

> An environmental injustice exists when members of disadvantaged, ethnic, minority or other groups suffer disproportionately at the local, regional (sub-national), or national levels from environmental risks or hazards, and/or suffer disproportionately from violations of fundamental human rights as a result of environmental factors, and/or denied access to environmental investments, benefits, and/or natural resources, and/or are denied access to information; and/or participation in decision making; and/or access to justice in environment-related matters.

We note in these definitions the important themes of information access and transparency, public participation, fairness, and equity. We also see that environmental injustice issues can be expressed both as "brown" (pollution) problems or "green" (resource extraction) problems. Environmental injustice thus occurs locally, regionally, and nationally; it also occurs internationally in a globalized world, as strong countries protect their own territories from degradation while pushing it onto more vulnerable ones. This is conceptually distinct from one country controlling and consuming another's natural resources with impunity because of power imbalances, as the West did in the great era of colonialism, although that dynamic remains in play.

It should be noted that this line of inquiry does not grapple with the much thornier question of whether the world's human population can ever achieve environmental justice on a global scale, given our exploding numbers and tremendous rate of consumption of the world's limited resources. Government and community leaders naturally seek to safeguard the best interests of the populations over which they have jurisdiction or which they seek to represent, so it is not surprising that they resist pollution and environmental degradation or choose to locate it where there is least political resistance. Poor communities may feel they have little choice about hosting such activities, or decide that the benefits in terms of jobs and revenue outweigh the costs in scarred landscapes, disease, and shortened life spans. As human beings search the globe for ever-scarcer materials to sustain our consumption and run out of places to dispose of the solid and toxic waste that we produce, the effort to achieve environmental justice starts to feel like aiming at a moving target: A problem pops up in a new location as soon as one has been resolved. Some argue that the problem is global capitalism, which requires constant growth and the resources to perpetuate itself.

We must thus recognize the difficulty in achieving distributive justice. As long as our society relies on landfills, coal-fired power plants, and animal feedlots, they will have to go somewhere, creating inequity that fuels tensions. The "Not in My Backyard" (NIMBY) phenomenon underscores the importance of the word "displacement." One country's clean-up often means another's toxic sludge, garbage incinerator, or nuclear waste repository; one community's victory spells another's bad news. "Locally undesirable land uses," or LULUs, are worldwide phenomena, unwelcome externalities of modern industrialization. As we begin this discussion of environmental justice as it relates to China, we should remind ourselves that these dynamics occur almost everywhere. What Chinese neighborhoods, municipalities, and the state itself are doing to resist and shift extractive industries and manufacturing plants is little different from what others have been doing for centuries. Moreover, middle-class urban Han Chinese, like elites throughout the world, tend to believe themselves superior to rural farmers, ethnic minorities, and the poor, whether consciously or unconsciously, and see themselves as deserving of higher standards of environmental quality. Racism and classism are worldwide problems. The main differences in the case of China are those of scale, impact, and rapidity, of the sheer size of China's global footprint, and of the Chinese state's willingness to be heavy-handed, sometimes even brutal, in the achievement of its goals.

ENVIRONMENTAL JUSTICE IN THE URBAN SETTING

Cities around the world struggle with where to dispose of household waste. New in China is the NIMBY-ism of the middle class, which is often heralded as a form of environmental awakening and emerging civil society, while less attention is given to where the harm goes when a community successfully resists. As the Chinese middle class finds its political voice and demands a better environment, the clean-up of urban cores often causes areas near or just outside city boundaries to receive greater amounts of pollution. One of the most highly contested environmental problems in China is disposal of garbage. Landfills are expected to fill completely within a few years and are the sources of noise and stench, large amounts of methane (a highly destructive greenhouse gas), and toxics that leach into local groundwater, while incinerators can disperse toxics into the air where they spread even more widely. China generates 250 million tons of municipal solid waste, or one quarter of the world's total, enough to fill a Great Pyramid (Vanacore 2012). According to the China Statistical Yearbook, by the end of 2012 the country had 540 landfills and 138 incinerators.

As the *New York Times'* Keith Bradsher wrote in his 2009 story, "China's incinerators loom as a global hazard," China has already surpassed the U.S. in overall production of household garbage. Provincial and local governments are now building incinerators as partial solutions to overflowing garbage dumps, but many of these are associated with the production of toxic emissions of dioxin, mercury, and cadmium. This affects local residents and also floats into the atmosphere where it can be measured around the world. Residents of the wealthy cities of Shanghai and Beijing have demanded high levels of pollution control, and some of those incinerators are up to international standards. Yet in the poorer interior of the country, dioxin emissions are permitted to be ten times higher than those in the European Union and mercury levels are dangerously high. If China does not soon take steps to limit these emissions, global dioxin levels could double.

Even in wealthier cities, unease about the use of incinerators is growing, not least in the capital city of Beijing, which produces nearly 20,000 tons of garbage a day and is set to exceed capacity in all 20 of its waste treatment plants. A wonderful film, "Beijing Besieged by Waste," chronicles one ordinary citizen's effort to follow trash trucks and see where it all goes. Facing limited land space, the Beijing municipal government adopted an aggressive three-year strategy to add ten new incinerator facilities within two years, increasing the city's waste incineration rate from less than 10 percent before 2009 to 70 percent by 2015. Planned incinerators have been met with widespread protests. For example, in 2009 residents of the university area in Northwest Beijing's Haidian District mobilized to oppose plans to build an incinerator at the unpopular and nearly full Liulitun landfill, already the source of much unpleasant stench and noise. Residents argued that an incinerator would produce dioxin, mercury, and other toxics, and were heartened when the Ministry of Environmental Protection spoke out against the idea and in favor of improved recycling. After citizens launched protests stretching over many months and brought a lawsuit that succeeded in raising pressure and publicity, the government abandoned plans for an incinerator at that location. Local officials connected to the landfill were imprisoned for corruption; one committed suicide while in detention. However, even as Liulitun fills to capacity, a replacement incinerator is planned for Dagong village on the Western border of the city, near several scenic districts, where 1,600 tons of garbage per day will be burned to reduce volume and generate electricity. The government claims that fewer people will be impacted at the new location and that there will be information available about the pollutants produced (China Radio International 2011). But what is most clear about this shift of location is that the farmers of Dagong do not have the political clout to resist this "locally undesirable land use."

Other victims of urban environmental injustice can also be found near city boundaries: They are the marginalized rural migrants who make up China's "floating population." Urbanization and the relaxation of the residence card system have created conditions for the mobility of millions of farmers who travel to cities in search of employment, most of which is temporary work in factories and construction sites or as nannies and housemaids. Because their status is semi-legal in that they do not have rights to health care, schooling, or other government services, and they have limited funds, they often live in temporary shelters in city outskirts or in makeshift dormitories near construction sites. Sanitation conditions are poor and access to health care restricted. Lacking sewage treatment plants, waste from their communities spills directly into waterways and is a source of serious pollution. These marginalized migrants often suffer environmental contamination from indoor coal-burning for heat and fuel, unclean water for drinking and washing, and overcrowded and uncomfortable living situations that promote the spread of disease. Now that waste transfer stations and incinerators are increasingly sited on city outskirts, the migrant poor also bear the brunt of the toxic pollution, noise, and unsanitary conditions. While China's urban slums are nowhere near the scale of those of some cities in India or Brazil, this is in part because the government periodically rounds up the migrants, demolishes their homes and makeshift schools, and attempts to make them return from whence they came. However, there are few paid jobs back home, and life from farming remains at a subsistence level, so these migrants continue to eke out a hard existence as a marginalized underclass that supports China's growth and the lifestyles of the urban middle class. This mimics the rural-to-urban migration patterns of much of the developing world, but China's migration restrictions complicate legal and human rights matters even as they purport to combat an avalanche of slums. Acknowledging the depth of the problem, China's leaders have promised to reform the temporary residence card system, but as long as living standards and economic opportunities in major cities continue to entice China's poor, these problems are likely to persist.

As cities attempt to clean up their urban cores by relocating landfills and shutting and shifting polluting factories such as the PX factories that residents of Xiamen, Dalian, and Ningbo fought so successfully, these manufacturing facilities are often moved to peri-urban areas where members of the floating population can pick up poorly paid work and local entrepreneurs and officials can continue to earn profits, often while flouting environmental regulations. As Bai Xuemei (2008) writes, "Many cities are relocating their most polluting industries outside their boundaries. Although these cities are subsequently praised by the central government for their improved inner-city environmental quality, often the only real change is that the offending industries and their associated pollution are simply moved to neighboring cities or to surrounding rural areas." That was the case during the lead-up to the 2008 Olympics, which saw the government strenuously clean up the air in order to deliver on its promises to the

International Olympic Committee, and during and after the "APEC blue" 2014 summit.

ENVIRONMENTAL JUSTICE AT THE URBAN-RURAL DIVIDE: CANCER VILLAGES AND OTHER DISEASE CLUSTERS

We have discussed the horrific phenomenon of cancer villages in previous chapters. These are rural communities located near highly polluting chemical factories where cancer and other diseases are so highly concentrated that entire families are known to grow sick and die. In 2009 the journalist Deng Fei published an online map of China's "cancer villages" (listed under Additional Resources at the end of this chapter) which are found in almost every province. The map is readily accessible and details about each village are available in Chinese. The map shows the locations of more than 100 cancer villages, but many suspect that the real figure is many times higher. The high levels of cancer are associated with the presence of factories, often those making goods for export. It was not until the spring of 2013 that the government acknowledged the existence of such villages, but now the connection between high cancer rates and economic growth is widely acknowledged and the villages have been the subjects of anthropological investigation (Lora-Wainwright 2014).

While these cancer villages tend to be concentrated near wealthy cities in China's East, where international businesses have invested in joint ventures and manufacturing plants to take advantage of cheap labor and lax environmental laws, they are also emerging in the less developed West, where jobs are scarce and information about pollution is difficult to obtain. In Northeast Yunnan's Xinglong, for example, where an industrial park's paper mills and chemical factories discharge effluent into the river and fumes into the air, residents told the *Guardian*'s Jonathan Watts (2010a), "Before the factories were built, there was no cancer ... Now we hear every year that this person or that person has cancer, especially lung and liver cancer." A tenth of the village's goats died.

Cancer villages in the wealthy East have tended to be in poor counties near major cities and at the deltas of the Yellow, Yangzi, and Pearl Rivers, while inland they are clustered near rivers. Geographer Liu Lee's systematic study of cancer villages (2010) identifies media and Internet reports on 459 cancer villages, with every province except Tibet and Qinghai containing at least a few; sources include the influential China Central Television. The cancer clusters are most intense in poor farming villages where highly polluting industries are located. Liu writes,

> There seems to be a spatial pattern of environmental injustice in the cancer-village belt, for the location of cancer villages within and between provinces. . . . China has made major efforts in environmental protection in the past decades, including the establishment of eco-communities and model environmental cities; however, the cancer villages prove that China's efforts are only partially successful. . . . The rich, some of whom got rich through the polluting factories, live in better environmental conditions, while poor farmers live by the factories and suffer from the pollution on a daily basis.

The notorious Huai River basin has produced some of the worst cases: In the whole of China, the county of Shenqiu in Northwest Henan has the most cancer villages. One of these, Huangmengying, a village of only 2,400 people, saw 118 die in the decade between 1994 and 2004, half from cancer; 80 percent of young people are constantly ill. In some of these villages, the death rate is higher than the birth rate, and villagers are heavily in debt because of medical bills (the documentary "Warriors of Qiugang," mentioned in Chapter Five, portrays a cancer village in the Huai River basin, in Anhui Province).

Other rural environmental justice problems occur in villages near battery smelters, where widespread lead poisoning has left almost all of the local children with cognitive and developmental problems. Similar problems are caused by cadmium and mercury contamination stemming from poorly managed recycling of electronic waste shipped to China from Europe and North America, as discussed more fully later in this chapter. Human Rights Watch (2011a) alleges that the impact of these toxic wastes has been covered up and tests falsified by the government.

What identifies these problems as issues of environmental justice is that the residents of these villages are largely poor and sometimes illiterate, with limited ability to organize politically, use the legal system, or seek redress. We saw in the last chapter how heroic groups have stepped in to help these people seek justice, despite harassment and even arrests, including Wang Canfa's Center for Legal Assistance to Victims of Pollution, Green Anhui, Huo Daishan's group the Huai River Defenders, and the Chongqing Green Volunteers Alliance. We have also seen how Greenpeace's undercover efforts to track effluents from shoe and apparel manufacturers have caused international businesses to promise to stop dumping toxics into China's waterways.

ENVIRONMENTAL JUSTICE BETWEEN CHINA'S EAST AND WEST

Some of the most poignant Chinese examples of environmental injustice can be found between the developed coastal areas and the peripheral, largely minority-occupied Western regions, which are rich in natural resources such as fossil fuels, minerals, timber, and rivers that can be dammed to produce hydroelectric power. This complicated dynamic requires us to reflect on the nature of the state itself, and then to plumb specific examples of these vast, but comparatively less populated areas.

One of the state's primary functions is the extraction of resources, with environmental degradation as a common by-product. This phenomenon is far from new. For centuries the less developed Western and frontier areas of China have seen the state try to secure resource-rich territory for exploitation for use by the developed coastal areas. Stevan Harrell (1995) has described how such efforts have been framed in a discourse of "civilizing," "liberating," "developing," and "modernizing" a "backwards" people for their own good. In recognition of problems in its handling of Han-minority relations and out of concern for the increasing wealth gap between China's rich and poor, in 1999 the state launched a "Develop the West" or "Open up the West" campaign [xibu da kaifa 西部大开发]. The program is officially intended to decrease severe economic inequalities between the coastal areas and the hinterlands. Critics argue that this campaign may also be motivated by a wish to maintain social stability. As the central core in the East grows wealthy, those on the periphery are left behind and grow increasingly resentful, posing challenges to Beijing's authority. Whatever the underlying motivation, critics say this campaign, with its focus on infrastructure investments such as roads, railroads, dams, and power plants, primarily facilitates resource extraction that benefits coastal areas and produces only nominal benefits for local populations.

The spatial displacement of environmental harm to contested "autonomous" regions on China's periphery such as Xinjiang, Inner Mongolia, Tibet, Qinghai, and Ningxia, and to provinces like Gansu and Yunnan, shares common patterns. Resources are exploited in places where local ethnic minority people who have nominal power to govern themselves tend to be excluded from the benefits of such exploitation. While some of these provinces are officially "autonomous," they have little self-governing power; Jonathan Watts describes them ironically as places where people are "free to do anything Beijing likes" (2010b, p. 208). Historically, state-organized activities have led to an increase in such environmental problems as deforestation, erosion, inappropriate land use, desertification, nuclear waste, and increased population pressures on local ecosystems. In these regions, political repression and extractive activities have been closely linked (Shapiro 2001).

This situation reminds us of one of our core questions: Can China deal with the acute poverty in much of the country, even as parts of the nation grow rich? Or do poverty-alleviation programs end up masking and contributing to a dynamic of environmental and political exploitation, sometimes even despite the best of intentions of policy makers? The various ethnic minority border regions have their own histories due to vastly different geographies and cultural traditions, so we will focus on just two well-known examples: Inner Mongolia and Tibet.

Inner Mongolia

The Inner Mongolian Autonomous Region (to be distinguished from Mongolia, an independent country) was a target for post-Liberation "settling the border" campaigns. Han Chinese were encouraged to move to the frontiers in multiple waves to civilize restive ethnic minority nationalities like the Mongols, whose nomadic lifestyles were considered backwards. This state-building effort to relocate Han to the borders culminated during the Cultural Revolution with a campaign to mobilize against the Soviet Union and also to grow cereals in a "grain first" effort to "Prepare against war, Prepare against famine, Serve the people." The campaign reflected China's deep insecurity about food supply during the years immediately following the 1959–61 state-induced famine (Becker 1997; Dikötter 2010). This effort to convert grasslands into farmland during the 1970s, chronicled in Ma Bo's memoir, translated into English as *Blood Red Sunset* (1996), was ultimately abandoned after the ecological damage became apparent and many Han were permitted to return home to the cities. At that point, the emphasis shifted to herding, with additional disastrous consequences from overgrazing, leading the state to shift to promote farming, livestock pens, and mining.

Nowadays, traditionally nomadic Mongol herders are being moved to urban centers as part of an "ecological migration" policy adopted in 2001. The government argues that nomadism and overgrazing are responsible for the degradation of the grasslands and the expansion of the desert, which now lies only four hours from the capital. The sandstorms that originate here sweep Beijing and can drift as far away as Japan and Korea, and even to the U.S. and Canadian West Coasts. In truth, the government may be more interested in securing access to grasslands to expand mining, commercial ranching and farming to satisfy the appetites of China's newly wealthy, and therefore is using "ecological migration" as a convenient excuse to eradicate traditional ethnic ways of living that may challenge Han authority. As scholar James Scott has pointed out in his important book, *Seeing Like a State* (1998), the ideology of modernization often leads states to use authoritarian means to reconfigure populations for state-building purposes.

The environmental damage the state attributes to the nomads has also in large part been created by past policies of the central government. When concern for the environment (and for minority cultures) is low on the list of state priorities, enormous damage and disruption can be inflicted in a relatively short period of time. In the late 1950s, herders were pushed into "People's Communes," large-scale economic and social institutions designed to speed up China's social and political transformation toward socialism. Then, in the rush to dismantle the communes in the post-Mao era, the land and herds were split up, and assigned and contracted to individual families. The government failed to recognize that grazing requires flexibility to adjust and adapt to climatic variability, and combining herds may be highly efficient, since only a small number of shepherds are required to monitor a herd. Local people resisted attempts to replace goats and sheep with penned cattle, for indigenous Mongols regard the nomadic lifestyle as an integral part of their cultural identity, as described powerfully in Jiang Rong's *Wolf Totem* (2008).

Government officials ignored indigenous knowledge and traditional practices which had helped to maintain an ecological balance in the past. Local herders could have told them that wolves play a key role in preserving the ecological balance of the grasslands, and that corralled animals that can smell fresh grass will not eat hay and thus starve at the very moment that their strength is needed most for lambing. Similarly, when the government attempted to restore sections of the grassland, officials ignored the need for livestock paths to get at water and forage. As a result, poor and disenfranchised villagers have ended up employing what James Scott (1985) calls "weapons of the weak" to dodge enforcement, grazing their animals at night to avoid detection, hiding animal numbers by cooperating with one another to exceed per-household quotas, and paying off local officials (Wang, Xiaoyi 2007). Yet the state insists that it knows what is best for the local people even as they protest that their very identities are under assault. Environmental protection is being used as a banner to bring frontier populations into eco-modernity, even though sought-for environmental improvements are widely acknowledged as unattained (Yeh 2009).

Meanwhile, intensive mining has become a source of tension between indigenous Mongols and the mining companies that have hastened to take advantage of the great demand for coal and the "rare earth" elements, of which China controls a near-monopoly, used in electronics, solar panels, and high-tech defense equipment. Inner Mongolia now supplies one quarter of China's massive consumption of coal, in part because reserves lie near the surface and are relatively easy to extract, a powerful draw in a country where the underground mining industry is the most dangerous in the world. Conflicts with herders have resulted. For example, in May 2011, two Mongol herdsmen who were trying to keep their traditional grazing grounds from being polluted and destroyed were killed, one of them run over by a truck and another killed during a protest over pollution. Their deaths sparked further protests and short-term government imposition of martial law. Dru Gladney, an anthropologist who studies Chinese minorities, told the *Los Angeles Times'* David Pierson that such conflicts between coal and grassland "are tinderbox issues for the Mongols. They do not think they are always benefiting from the resources being extracted" (2011). As more traditional grazing land is fenced off for mines, similar conflicts can be expected to become more frequent.

In Inner Mongolia, the state initially distorted sustainable human–nature balances and traditional grassland use by promoting in-migration and land transformation in order to grow grain, and then justified heavy-handed interference with local culture through the use of an environmental protection discourse. In the name of "ecological resettlement," nomads are prevented from allowing their animals to roam freely and are forced to move into towns and cities where the state can control them more easily, even as mining companies move to exploit the rich reserves beneath the grasslands. The use of the grasslands as a sustainable resource is essentially a memory of the past, since desertification is one of the most difficult forms of environmental degradation to reverse. The state's heavy investment in "Green Belt" afforestation and reforestation projects, which began shortly after the 1949 revolution and have intensified in recent years as desertification inches toward Beijing, have had only mixed results over the decades. At the present moment, the state has combined its disparate goals of ecological protection and assertion of Han-style national identity: Using environmental protection as a pretext for suppression of ethnic identities perceived to threaten national unity, the state has forced herders to get out of the way of mining companies, some of which are large multinational investors from Australia and elsewhere. In terms of environmental injustice, ethnic minorities whose very identities are tied up in traditional uses of the landscape have suffered grievously as a result of degradation and overuse from which they have received little benefit.

Tibet

Greater Tibet (which includes the Tibetan Autonomous Region and parts of Gansu, Sichuan, Qinghai, and Yunnan) provides another poignant example of China's problems with dramatic environmental injustice in border regions. As in other frontier areas, the state plays a leading role in resource extraction and environmental degradation as well as repression of local cultures and national identities. Extreme as the damage already is, the greatest destruction likely lies in the future. The railroad between low-lying Golmud in Qinghai Province and the Tibetan capital of Lhasa was completed only in 2006, and more railroads are in the planning stages. Despite the fanfare about the development benefits the railroad will bring to Tibet, it is also expected to bring an increase in extraction of precious metals and minerals and an influx of Han migrants, who will outnumber local Tibetans in the foreseeable future. Multiple new airports will further facilitate Han control of the region and consolidate military power along the contested border with India. Such infrastructure development will effectively render impotent Tibetan efforts to contest Chinese claims of sovereignty.

China's treatment of Tibet illustrates how history, politics, state security, and a lack of respect for indigenous cultures can combine with devastating impact on the environment. China's claim to Tibet is based on a brief period in the distant past during the Tang dynasty (618–907), when Chinese princess Wen Cheng was married to Tibetan king Songtsen Gampo. Following the 1949 revolution and the founding of the People's Republic, China "liberated" Tibet from the rule of the Dalai Lama, claiming a role as liberator of a feudal society in which corrupt monks extracted wealth from a backwards people. An attempted uprising in 1959 was forcibly suppressed, and the Dalai Lama escaped into exile in Northern India. This story and these competing claims to Tibet are well told in a book by John Avedon, *In Exile from the Land of Snows* (1984) and in the Dalai Lama's own memoir, *Freedom in Exile* (1990).

The impact of China's exploitation of Tibetan resources will be felt throughout Asia. Many of the great rivers of Asia rise in the Tibetan Plateau, including the Indus, Brahmaputra, Yangzi, Yellow, Salween (Nu), and Mekong. Dams and global warming will affect the Himalayan ice fields that feed the rivers, which will have an impact on China as well as surrounding countries. Industrial pollution of the headwaters could prove disruptive well beyond the "roof of the world", sparking fears in India and elsewhere of "water wars" (Chellaney 2013). Such degradation will be tragic given the traditional Tibetan commitment to sustainability, with cultural and religious beliefs forbidding the unnecessary killing of animals, pollution of water, disruption of soil, and excessive logging (Lowe 1992, Yeh 2014).

Much environmental degradation in Greater Tibet has already occurred. Many old-growth forests were cut during the decades after the Communist victory in 1949. Although logging in western China was banned in 1998 after the government recognized that widespread soil erosion was contributing to heavy flooding downstream, illegal deforestation continues. Grasslands have already been severely degraded both in the Tibetan Autonomous Region itself and in traditionally Tibetan areas in Gansu, Qinghai, and Sichuan. In 2009, state-media agency *Xinhua* reported Chinese officials as acknowledging desertification in Tibet proper to be spreading by almost 100,000 *mu* (one mu = about 0.16 acres) a year. Some scholars believe this degradation is essentially desertification wrought by climate change, although not all agree (Gao et al. 2006; Harris 2010).

Until the completion of the railroad connecting Xining and Lhasa, China's determination to conquer and hold Tibet could best be explained by the state's perceived need for a buffer between China and India, with which it has had hostile relations for decades. The disputed border between China and India remains politically unresolved in part because of Chinese difficulty with supply lines. The railroad will allow China to confront India with much greater ease and may change the power equation. The railroad does not merely alter the geo-strategic political calculus, however. It can also be seen as a way of drawing Tibet and its rich mineral and water resources into the bosom of China proper, permitting industry to locate there for the first time. While Tibetans traditionally do not mine because they believe doing so takes from the earth's strength, the Chinese are eager to exploit the 126 identified minerals to be found there, which include uranium, lithium, chromite, boron, borax, iron, gold, copper, silver, and zinc, as well as oil and gas. Moreover, China plans to build more than 750 dams, including one near the ethnic Tibetan city of Deqen in Yunnan, on the Upper Yangzi, which would replace the massive dam planned for Tiger Leaping Gorge which was canceled after intense efforts by local farmers and Beijing activists. In Tibet proper, a hydropower station site at Yamdrok Yumtso, a large holy lake believed to contain the spirit of Tibet, is guarded by 1,500 Chinese People's Liberation Army troops. The dam will provide electricity for Lhasa, which has increasingly become a Han city that serves as an overflow valve for excess population from the East (Moore 2008). Finally, China's plans for Greater Tibet include the planned Western route for the South-North Water Transfer, a highly controversial and technically difficult engineering feat which, if accomplished, would have major ecological impacts on the Tibetan plateau as well as Southwestern rivers like the Mekong and Salween that drain into Southeast Asia. The "land of snows" that once seemed so alien and forbidding, where Han were sent only for hardship posts, has now become so Sinicized that Han are beginning to find it an attractive relocation option.

Tibet, along with other Western ethnic minority regions like Yunnan, has also been heavily influenced by millions of Han Chinese tourists, who once could not dream of traveling for vacation. Now, with disposable income for the first time, they are on the move. Such regions have captured the popular imagination as romantic destinations for ecotourism and ethnotourism. As in other minority regions, with the motive for profit dominating, tourists are "consuming" both people and nature. Entrepreneurs from as far away as Shenzhen near Hong Kong are buying up ethnic products, shops, and small inns in minority regions, so much that this has affected local artists' choices about what to produce and profoundly distorted local culture. Tour groups are taken to minority villages, where local people dressed in traditional costume perform welcome ceremonies and offer music, dance, traditional crafts, and lunch. The commodification of culture also extends to the great monasteries of Tibet that were once the crown jewels of Tibetan history and culture, in the style of universities. Now these places of worship and study are under tight military control and all but emptied of the tens of thousands of monks who once learned and practiced Tibetan Buddhism there. Tourist groups interrupt the sacred rituals and devotional practices of those who remain, and there is great political tension between monks and authorities. To accommodate more tourists, authorities have suggested building a "mini Potala" on a nearby hill. Meanwhile, in traditionally Tibetan areas in Western Sichuan and Northern Yunnan, national parks such as Napahai and Jiuzhaigou are being transformed into profit centers. Rather than continuing to permit a fluid boundary system in which local people can sustainably use and profit from the reserves, officials are experimenting with a Western-style system of "fortress conservation" with impermeable boundaries, high ticket prices, and tourist access through government controlled buses. Local people who once generated income by providing local lodging and horse rides are being excluded. In some cases, they are even forced to move outside park boundaries and forbidden from pursuing traditional light subsistence activities.

The Voice of America reported that on July 19, 2011, then-Vice-president Xi Jinping pledged to speed up Tibet's economic development and to promote the idea that Han and minorities "cannot live without each other." Speaking in Lhasa in front of the Potala Palace at a ceremony marking the 60th anniversary of Chinese rule, he praised Tibet as a national security bulwark, referring to its role as a barrier between China and India, as a place of ecological importance as the source of China's major rivers, and as a source of strategic resources. A few weeks later, young monk Tsewang Norbu from Ganzi County, a Tibetan region of Sichuan, drank gasoline, poured it over himself and burned himself to death as he shouted, "We Tibetans Want Freedom, Long Live the Dalai Lama." It was the second such desperate measure within a few months. Advocates have reported that 138 Tibetans have burned themselves to death or attempted to do so as of April 2015.

As we see from the examples of Inner Mongolia and Tibet, the Chinese state's projects of nation-building, cultural reordering, and resource extraction are intimately entwined. The result is often problems with environmental injustice in situations where alternative identities and ethnic allegiances are perceived as threats to the dominance of the Han Chinese. As it has struggled to do for centuries (Harrell 1995), Beijing is trying to bring these regions more tightly under the sway of the central state. Ethnic minorities are rewarded for playing by the rules and integrating into the dominant culture even as their traditional practices are depicted as backward and uncivilized. Beijing has provided a system of limited benefits through Minorities Institutes and favorable policies on birth quotas, as well as a "Develop the West" policy whose impacts are debatable. The state's motivations have not only been to establish clear boundaries and buffers against potential and perceived enemies and competitors, but also to secure access to resources, including grain-lands, hydropower, minerals, fossil fuels, and timber. Local people have had little say in whether and how these resources are used, and have seen little benefit from their extraction. In a clear and striking example of the dynamics of environmental injustice, the harms from degradation due to resource extraction have been displaced to the periphery, while environmental benefits have been enjoyed at the center.

The gaps between rich and poor, between Han and minorities, between interior and coast, are thus rooted in ethnicity, class, and above all access to resources. Whether these contradictions can be resolved will greatly affect China's prospects for "sustainable" development. A government committed to pursuing sustainable development must attempt to improve living standards without poisoning the country. It must attempt to demonstrate to ethnic minority groups that the national project does not disenfranchise them. It must pursue environmental equity, transparency, and the rule of law. These are serious challenges for any government, especially in a world reaching the limits of its resources.

Unfortunately, if trends continue, the government's stated purpose, that of achieving both environmental protection and economic growth, will be little more than a cloak for repression and environmental injustice in resource-rich border areas. There is little internal debate about this, perhaps because even many thoughtful and well-educated Han Chinese tend to believe the official line that the central government has done a great deal to help these "backwards" areas; they see minorities who protest or "riot" as simply ungrateful. Educated young Han eager for travel adventure hold romantic notions about life in Tibet and Inner Mongolia, but few have much understanding of the complexity or desirability of creating a multi-ethnic society that respects cultural difference without stereotyping, exploitation, or condescension. Moreover, few of them appreciate their own roles in perpetuating such dynamics.

ENVIRONMENTAL JUSTICE: INTERNATIONAL DIMENSIONS

We now turn to the international dimensions of environmental justice, with China serving as both an importer and exporter of environmental harm. In recent decades, the trend toward state-led environmental degradation has intensified and internationalized, as China's thirst for resources, from timber and wildlife to fossil fuels and minerals, has led to an increase in environmental degradation in places within and beyond national boundaries. We have already seen that as the world's manufacturing hub, China has attracted and borne the costs of pollution for many developed countries and that increasingly, within China, pollution is being pushed out of wealthy Eastern cities and into rural areas and the vulnerable West. While many international corporations argue that they adhere to more stringent environmental and labor standards than do Chinese domestic companies, anti-globalization activists claim that the developing world is in a "race to the bottom" as they compete against each other for foreign capital. By 2011, according to the Chinese Statistical Yearbook, foreign-owned companies accounted for 13.4 percent of industrial output; with foreign investment or joint ventures included, the total is 25.9 percent. Debate over whether such enterprises are generally positive or negative for China's environmental performance remains unresolved, with some evidence suggesting that much depends on whether the multinational corporations originate from low-standard or high-standard countries (Stalley 2010). When the problem of subcontracting to middlemen is included, as already mentioned with respect to the shoe and iPad manufacturers targeted by Greenpeace, it becomes even more difficult to make judgments on these firms' environmental impact. Such subcontractors are often from Hong Kong or Taiwan and have been associated with sweatshop-like conditions and substandard pollution controls.

As we reflect on how environmental harm is displaced to the vulnerable, we would be remiss not to consider one of the most dramatic examples of how the West exports some of its toxic materials to China in the form of post-consumer waste. The electronics recycling business, which is centered in a cluster of four small villages in southern Guangdong Province near Hong Kong, has some of the highest concentrations of toxic materials in the world. This is an issue of wide discussion and mobilization for the international environmental community.

The Basel Action Network (BAN) is a non-governmental organization dedicated to exposing the environmental injustices inherent in the globalization of the toxic waste trade, and is based on the 1989 Basel Convention on the Control of Transboundary Movements of Hazardous Wastes and Their Disposal. BAN activists have been working for more than a decade to stop the export of electronic wastes to China, especially from the United States (The U.S. has signed but not ratified the Basel Convention). International awareness of the e-waste problem was raised significantly in 2008 when CBS broadcast an episode of "60 Minutes" about the impact of this trade on the villages of Guiyu. The villages, which once produced rice, have become a dumping ground for the world's electronic detritus. The waste arrives by the containerload via Hong Kong. Villagers disassemble and sort components from computers, televisions, cell phones, and other electronics. Many of the chemicals are highly toxic, especially when burned or soaked in acid baths during the deconstruction. Small children and even babies play in mountains of waste as their parents extract minuscule quantities of copper, gold, chips, and other valuables for a meager living. Dioxin levels in Guiyu are the world's highest, while lead, chromium, tin, PVC flame retardants (which contain dioxin and furan), and other toxics also leach into the groundwater and fall from the air. Although laws in the U.S. and other developed countries as well as China forbid the export and import of these materials, and virtuous citizens in the West often go to great lengths to ensure that their toxic electronics are disposed of in what they believe to be a responsible fashion, the illegal trade is highly lucrative and loopholes abound. Indeed, Greenpeace estimates that 50 to 80 percent of U.S. e-waste is exported, much of it to Asia, although Africa also gets its share. The U.S. EPA is cooperating with China and other developing countries to reduce the trade and find a solution (http://epa.gov/oia/toxics/ewaste.html). Greenpeace, BAN, and other NGOs are pressuring electronics manufacturers to stop using the most hazardous substances in their products and have obtained commitments from some of them. However, as the worldwide consumption of electronic products continues to explode, and the lifetimes of these products grow ever shorter with the introduction of must-have gadgets that make usable products appear to be obsolete, this problem is likely to worsen.

International impacts

Thus far, this book has been focused primarily on how China's environmental challenges are playing out domestically. The themes we have identified in earlier chapters suggest a need for further research into how they play out in the international arena, as the country and its businesses engage, operate, and develop elsewhere in the world. How do domestic considerations affect the role of the Chinese government on the world stage? How does Chinese national identity fuel its international actions? How and where is civil society within China making transnational linkages? Moreover, in terms of environmental justice and the displacement of environmental harm, we cannot ignore the external environmental consequences of China's explosive economic growth and efforts to curb environmental degradation at home. Decades ago, China was largely isolated from the world; today Chinese foreign aid programs and businesses are active worldwide, and the sheer size of China's global environmental footprint in an age of globalization and massive capital flow dwarfs anything the world has seen before.

On the subject of China's international impact, some observers hold a largely positive view. They argue, for example, that Chinese aid projects are rebuilding Africa across multiple sectors, providing for schools and roads as well as energy and resources infrastructure (Brautigam 2009). Although a number of investments seem aimed at procuring resources, other projects, such as hospitals, are not as clearly directed at extraction. Chinese foreign aid balance sheets can be opaque, but broad economic and strategic interests appear to remain at the heart of many of China's decisions, some of which are resource oriented, some of which are not. Nonetheless, it is clear that many projects in Latin America, Africa, and the Middle East are focused on securing resources and energy (Dittmer and Yu 2010, Economy and Levi 2014). This may be a case of China's self-interests in markets and materials aligning with the needs of less developed countries for investment and capital. Perhaps as a response to criticisms that China is primarily interested in shoring up strategic resources across the globe, the government in 2011 released a white paper demonstrating that only about 5% of its development projects are directly related to oil and mining, while more than half focus on economic infrastructure and public facilities. This is consistent with the Chinese contention that foreign aid should be mutually beneficial (Kjøllesdal and Welle-Strand 2010). This point also drew praise from analysts at the Worldwatch Institute (Bi 2011), who hailed China's approach as a "green aid" model for the world.

A darker viewpoint suggests that China's overseas development assistance projects are largely focused, if subtly so, on gaining access to resources. That was the conclusion of the Congressional Research Service (Lum et al. 2009), based on an earlier, widely cited review by the Robert F. Wagner Graduate School of Public Service at New York University. Critics suggest that China is engaging in a modern version of colonialism, offering foreign aid to build infrastructure like roads and deep-water ports to allow for easier extraction of resources. Seeking to assure a steady supply of primary materials, Chinese state-owned companies have invested heavily in infrastructure like roads and deep ports, often in the name of foreign aid. Some of these projects are funded with private capital, usually with strong government ties; a Chinese businessman with murky connections plans to build a channel across Nicaragua to rival the Panama Canal.

Some Chinese business investments, as distinct from the government's foreign aid packages, point alarmingly to resource grabbing. According to Chinese Ministry of Commerce statistics for 2014, Chinese outward direct investment (ODI) was $102.89 billion, among the highest in the world. China's growth rate in ODI continues to outpace the growth rate of FDI it attracts into China; an official from the Commerce Ministry predicts that China will soon become a net capital exporter. Much of that was by government-owned or -controlled entities, with investment in the energy, materials, and mining sectors remaining key targets. The overall impact of this activity is transforming landscapes everywhere.

China's extraction of raw materials such as timber, grain, fossil fuels, and minerals is stunning in its effects on the planet. Such extraction provides raw materials for China's domestic consumption needs, but it also provides raw materials for the massive manufacturing project China has undertaken to meet global consumption demands. Control of raw materials is also considered a good business investment by Chinese institutions and individuals looking for a place to invest their enormous wealth. As more Chinese enjoy higher incomes and demand a better standard of living, government and industry are casting about the globe for food, material inputs, economic partners, and markets. At the same time, China's own increasingly stringent environmental standards – particularly the country's celebrated, if also flouted, logging ban – have decreased damaging activities domestically, shifting pressure to other countries. As was discussed earlier, China's furniture manufacturing industry still needs lumber and seeks it from forests abroad. Moreover, some provinces under pressure to clean up their air pollution are actively seeking to relocate dirty factories overseas, a new phenomenon dubbed "dirty migration."

To facilitate these investments, and despite U.S. opposition, China has led the BRICS countries to set up a New Development Bank to counter the influence of the dollar and the World Bank and IMF, with the promise of providing credit for infrastructure projects in the developing world (the U.K. and Australia have also joined). Other innovative financing mechanisms include the much-criticized "loans for oil" deals that have been signed with the governments of Angola, Ecuador, and Venezuela. We will now examine several examples of the environmental impacts of China's global resources quest.

Ecuador, in a difficult financial position after defaulting on its loans in 2008, began trading oil for Chinese loans in 2009. Heavily dependent on Chinese credit, the Correa government in 2013 concluded an agreement that gives drilling rights to Petro China to extract oil from beneath the highly biodiverse and sensitive Yasuni National Park in the Amazon rainforest. This is a UNESCO Biosphere Reserve that is home to the Huaorani and other indigenous groups, two of them uncontacted. The deal has been roundly criticized, not only because the region is a crown jewel of global biodiversity but also because negotiations were conducted while the government claimed to be trying to raise international donations to put the Reserve off limits to drilling. The deal is worth an initial billion in favorable credit for Ecuador from the China Development Bank, secured by oil to be sold at a fixed price. It is one of the starkest illustrations of China's willingness to step in where other nations hold back because of civil society pressure and public opinion about justice and indigenous rights. The China Development Bank has been active throughout Latin America and Africa, providing generous credit in exchange for guaranteed access to resources, often in regions where corruption and/or political unrest make them the only game in town (Sanderson and Forsythe 2013).

Mining is one of the world's most conflicted extractive industries and China has been associated with social unrest and environmental degradation in Africa and Latin America. In Zambia, the government announced in 2014 that it would take over the strife-ridden Collum copper mine, which had drawn attention from international human rights groups (Human Rights Watch 2011b). In Ghana, discontent runs high over small-scale illegal Chinese gold miners. In the DRC, however, fortune smiles on China: in a variant of the debt-for-oil model, a resources-for-infrastructure project financed by the China Development Bank has revived plans for a huge controversial iron and cobalt mine, Sicomines (Jansson 2013).

Chinese mining interests, particularly in iron ore and copper, are arguably most active in Peru. A new left-wing wave of resource extractivism is taking place in Latin America under the banner of funding government social programs, and national policies under Peru's President Humala actively favor foreign mining investment. Chinese companies are learning from the negative experience of the decades-old Shougang iron ore mine, notorious for strikes and worker discontent. The Chinese have often been poor at dealing with local citizens' groups because they assume that a government contract means the project will go forward, as has been their experience at home in ethnic minority regions like Inner Mongolia, Xinjiang, and Tibet, where mining usually proceeds with little local consultation, sometimes even in contravention of indigenous knowledge and spiritual practices. However, the Chinese aluminum corporation Chinalco successfully relocated the town of Morococha at the Toromocho copper mine to make way for an expansion. Activists had expected that moving the community would lead to widespread unrest, but the Chinese hired a specialized consulting firm that gained residents' trust and built a new town even better than the old. In 2014, China purchased Las Bambas, one of Peru's largest copper projects, from Glencore Xstrata, which had been repeatedly fined for environmental violations, in a seven billion dollar cash deal. Local activists are anxious: How the Chinese consortium, led by state-owned Minmetals, handles construction and community labor relations will show whether it has understood that failure to mitigate environmental impacts and gain community support is ultimately poor business practice. Also in Peru, additional impacts fan out from large projects like mines. In Northern Peru, Chinese buyers of maca, a ground-grown tuber thought to be an aphrodisiac, have sent prices skyward and brought crime and unexpected wealth to remote highland areas. The tubers are required under Peruvian law to be processed in the country, but smugglers are transporting them overland to Bolivia, and there is fear of seed-stealing and the eventual production of maca in China, with a loss of seed sovereignty to Peru (Neuman 2014).

As we provide further examples of China's international environmental impact, we must flag its role as a major player in the global rush to secure farmland. China is far from the only actor, as multinational agribusinesses lead the charge, but China's impact on farmland is felt worldwide, with the Ministry of Agriculture encouraging investors to identify friendly, stable, resource-rich countries as sources for wheat, soybeans, corn, and rice. As seen, China is particularly sensitive about grain supply; the country has been plagued by famine throughout its history, and during the Cultural Revolution, "Take Grain as the Key Link" was a dominant political campaign, as urban dwellers, young and old, were sent to the far reaches of the country to try to convert wetlands and fill in lakes to try to increase arable land and secure China's grain supply. Even after China's entry into the global capital system after Mao, it has been a point of national pride to try to be self-reliant in grain. The loss of arable land domestically to developers and urbanization has been so worrisome to policy makers that a "red line" of 120 million hectares was established in the 2006 11th Five-Year Plan, below which acreage of arable land should not drop. However, given increased attention to heavy-metal soil pollution (particularly the cadmium discovered in rice grown in Hunan) and China's "going out" policy, Chinese investors have understood that they can grow crops overseas. The conversion of forests to grainfields, and the dispossession and displacement of small farmers, is part of a global "land grab" that groups like the International Land Coalition, GRAIN, and farmland-grab.org are struggling to document and resist.

A final driver of the expansion of China's environmental footprint overseas is migration: the sheer number of Chinese seeking better economic opportunities (and political freedom) abroad is a testament to an adventurous, entrepreneurial spirit that is far from new (see, for example, the Chinese construction of America's Transcontinental Railroad). However, the ease with which ordinary Chinese can now get passports (rare if not impossible during the Mao period and subsequent decade), and their ability to fund their initial voyage, mean that Chinese small businesses can be found throughout the world, often in unlikely places such as Zambia, where Chinese entrepreneurs are harvesting old-growth redwoods (French 2014). Although Chinese may be no better or worse than poor people seeking to make a buck from other parts of the world, they seem unusually visible, inexperienced at respecting local customs, and willing to do whatever it takes to turn a profit. Chinese immigrants are not only highly active in industries like mining and fisheries, but they are even cornering the market on obscure commodities like lavender.

China's newfound economic clout, its enthusiasm for international investment encouraged and enabled by government policy and generous financing, and population outflow are transforming landscapes across the globe. Where others fear to tread, China marches in, often with large numbers of workers and support personnel. Where others hesitate to pursue an opportunity because of high prices or social and environmental concerns, China is ready with an open wallet. At a moment when the environmental transformation of the planet seems to be occurring at warp speed, China's funds, personnel, and investment philosophy act as catalysts and magnifiers. The rest of the world is often preoccupied with other concerns, and countries on the receiving end of so much Chinese attention have little context to understand their new suitor or time to absorb what it all means. Attention to environmental injustice on the global scale sensitizes us to the fact that poor countries are not in a position to resist when China comes courting, even when the resources they sell are not renewable, or when they give up legal rights to their own land and dispossess their most vulnerable people.

Geopolitical flashpoints with resources-securing aspects

Finally, we must note that China's resources push has sometimes raised geopolitical tensions. This is particularly evident in four cases, including dam-building, territorial claims to islands in offshore waters, claims to Arctic resources and shipping lanes projected to become available due to climate change, and oil and gas pipeline construction from Russia and Central Asia to East Asian ports. This section provides an overview of each of these potential flashpoints.

As noted, the Tibetan Plateau is home to the headwaters of most of the major rivers of South and Southeast Asia. Particularly contentious are dams already built or being built on the Mekong (in China, Lancang), and Salween (in China, Nu), as well as Chinese sponsorship of dams across the border in Laos and Burma. China is not a full member of the Mekong River Commission (intended to facilitate governance of the watershed), perhaps in an effort to avoid being bound by its authority. Domestic campaigns against dam-building in the Southwest part of China, as well as concerns about risks of dams built in seismically active regions (the 2008 Sichuan earthquake is one such example, with some experts arguing that the weight of the water caught above the Zipingbu dam may have caused "reservoir-induced seismicity"), have only sporadically delayed plans to make hydropower a central part of China's renewable energy portfolio. However, the countries of Southeast Asia have little power to resist the gigantic Chinese dam-building machine, although resistance to a Chinese dam planned for the Mekong in Myanmar was so widespread in 2011 that the Burmese government pulled back, a surprising move for an authoritarian country heavily beholden to China.

An even greater hydropower flashpoint may be in India's concerns about dams on the Brahmaputra, the first of which, the Zangmu, is already under construction. China and India remain in a contentious geopolitical relationship, with long stretches of the border disputed, while China's cozy relationship with Pakistan and cooperation on nuclear energy is another source of tension. China has attempted to reassure India that such dams will not have a significant impact downstream, but India remains highly suspicious of China's intentions (Chellaney 2013).

The most famous geopolitical flashpoint is doubtless the tensions over the Spratleys, Paracels and other islands in the South China Sea and the Senkaku (Diaoyu) islands in the Sea of Japan (East China Sea). While some argue that China's muscular claims have more to do with nationalism and settling historical scores than they do with resources, offshore oil and gas reserves are more accessible than ever due to new technologies. China has built an oil rig in the Paracels within an exclusive economic zone (EEZ) claimed by Vietnam, accompanied by PLA warships, and stepped up deep water oil and gas exploration in both disputed and undisputed waters. Moreover, the rich fishing grounds and shipping lanes of the region are an important resource, especially now that China has essentially fished out or poisoned the fish stocks near its clearly defined coastal EEZs, with an estimated 30 percent collapsed and another 20 percent severely stressed (Mallory 2013). Disputes over how EEZ lines should be drawn, which are especially tense with the Philippines and Vietnam, have led China to reject mediation efforts by the UN Convention on the Law of the Sea (UNCLOS), despite its status as a party. China claims that historical maps prove its ownership of the islands and the extensive EEZ rights that conveys. Because the U.S. has traditional security relationships in the region, particularly with the Philippines and Japan, these flashpoints are highly volatile, contentious, and dangerous.

China's 4,000-vessel distant water fleet (DWF) is often its first projection of military intentions in disputed waters and can be outfitted with sophisticated surveillance and navigation technologies. Boats that fish in territorial waters are often sufficient to set off international incidents. South Korea alone has captured almost 4,000 Chinese boats fishing in its waters since 2001. Anecdotal evidence points to China's practice of threatening to withdraw infrastructure aid programs if developing countries do not provide fisheries access and turn a blind eye to unsustainable practices such as "pair trawling," particularly in the coastal waters of West Africa, which has the most "illegal, unreported, and unregulated" fishing boats (IUUs) on earth. China now lands more wild fish than any other country. Peru, which sends almost all of its anchovy catch to China, comes in second (Blomeyer et al. 2012).

China's role in the Arctic, too, has potential for conflict. China is not an Arctic nation, yet sheer power earned it permanent observer status at the eight-member Arctic Council as of May 2013, together with India and Japan. Although decision-making still largely rests with the eight Arctic nations, China has made it clear that it considers itself a player. It has built an icebreaker and joined Arctic research institutions, while Chinese buyers claiming to be interested in building tourist facilities have been strangely active in Stavanger, in Norway's Arctic. Access to Arctic shipping lanes will shorten shipping times between Shanghai and Hamburg by 4,000 miles over the usual route via the Suez Canal. Moreover, the rich fishing grounds are of great interest, and China is attempting to keep as much area accessible as possible.

While so far the Arctic Council has been an amicable body, China has participated in tensions over Russia's claims over the extended continental shelf.

Finally, pipeline disputes are potential geopolitical flashpoints, particularly as China, Japan, and South Korea rival for Russian gas and oil, even as the pipelines are agents of environmental degradation in and of themselves. For example, the East Siberia–Pacific Ocean oil pipeline was embroiled in accusations that China had underpaid on its obligations, and the Gazprom monopoly has repeatedly obstructed China's efforts to gain access to Russian natural gas supplies. Eighty percent of China's gas now comes from the countries of Central Asia via an interlinked Central Asia–China pipeline, and these countries are prone to territorial disputes among themselves. Moreover, Sino-Japanese relations have reached new lows in recent years. These disputes center on territory and end-points for Russian pipelines, but they are fanned by the Japanese treatment of WWII in textbooks and Japanese leaders' visits to war dead shrines. To punish Japan, China has sometimes withheld exports of the rare earths over which it holds a near-monopoly, and which Japan desperately needs for manufacture of electronics, solar panels, and other technological applications.

In sum, China's quest for resources sometimes catalyzes geopolitical risk. Contested resources range from hydropower captured on transboundary watercourses, distant fisheries, shipping lanes, and oil and natural gas. While it is well established that resources competition is generally a contributor to conflict rather than a direct cause, China's relationships worldwide are clearly influenced, for better and worse, by the global race to secure resources in a shrinking world. The desire to capture resources can be seen in China's relationships with its immediate neighbors, with its historical rivals, and with its beneficiaries in the developing world. China's environmental footprint is thus not only a matter of supply and demand but also one of projection of hard power by a new global superpower. Whether this superpower will be able to wield its influence in a just and equitable manner remains to be seen.

As we have seen, China's environmental challenges shape broad world politics surrounding the environment and beyond. China's drive to secure basic raw materials for its production lines expresses itself through new funding and foreign aid mechanisms in the developing world as well as direct competition with developed countries on the open market. So rapid and aggressive is China's rise that its environmental issues have assumed geopolitical importance. The country's policymakers understand securing resources as a basic right to which China is entitled by virtue of historical unfairness and its current huge population and vast landmass. While many other countries have a huge "shadow ecology" that extends beyond their borders, none has seen so dramatic a change in such a short time, and none has the global reach to affect the economies and landscapes in the most remote places on earth. The most obscure commodities have changed fortunes when the Chinese spotlight shines, along with the ownership of global brands and extractive projects.

China's global environmental footprint is a moving target. The unimaginable has become possible; the possible has become likely and the likely is already in the past. Scholars of global environmental politics would do well to take heed. China claims to want to play by global rules, but it also claims to want to rewrite them, replacing the Washington Consensus with the China Consensus, supplementing the Bretton Woods Institutions with a developing world bank, challenging the dominance of the dollar. While Chinese environmentalists are among the world's bravest and most creative, the sheer magnitude of China's global reach limits their influence. It is essential that the world community involve China in the quest for global environmental governance such that the world's largest emerging economy can become a champion of norms of justice and sustainability.

We can see the potential for positive outcomes from China's development strategies abroad if host countries do indeed benefit from increases in aid, trade, and investment. Yet China's economic demands also present grave challenges for environmental justice. Opening new markets and tapping resources may benefit China and its partner nations in the short run; however, they also lead to environmental degradation, as well as a tendency to flood local markets with cheap consumer goods and crowd out subsistence local traders. The spreading of the Chinese development model, which is not so different from previous centuries of Western-led development, raises serious concerns: Can the world sustain this? Can the planet survive such demand and conquest? Who are the winners, who are the losers? One of the most important ways that we can answer this question is by refraining from painting China as all good or all bad. We must cultivate a nuanced appreciation for China's historical moment, constraints, pressures, and ambitions, and for the responsibilities of other countries. Only then are equitable solutions likely to emerge.

CONCLUSIONS

As we have seen in this chapter, the dynamics of environmental injustice tend to push the costs of pollution onto the most vulnerable and politically weak. A well-organized anti-pollution push in one place can result in a factory opening somewhere else. Pressure to clean Beijing's air has shifted industry to outlying areas and diverted resources from other projects. Rural areas become dumping grounds for urban waste. Poor countries bear the brunt of pollution for wealthy consumers. Broadly speaking, environmental harms tend to be displaced from wealthy areas to poor ones, even as resources are extracted disproportionately from remote and less developed areas to fuel economic growth for more developed countries, including China. As these tensions and contradictions become more evident in a shrinking, globalizing world of limited resources, they are focusing increasing attention on the challenge of achieving environmental justice while providing for the needs of the world's growing population.

As we conclude this section on environmental justice, we may wish once again to raise questions asked at the beginning of this volume: Can this trend be reversed in a world of increasing limits of resources, even as pollution "sinks," including carbon repositories like forests, are shrinking quickly? Is it even possible to build a fair and equitable world? As China's story tells us, there are signs of hope, but also room for despair. China's demand for resources is being driven not only by domestic consumers but also by international ones. As the world's manufacturing engine, China bears some of the pollution costs of the developed world's overconsumption along with the consumption and waste generated by its own rising middle class. At the same time, China has only just begun to address the material needs of the impoverished periphery in its West. For these reasons, and despite strong environmental laws and regulations, Chinese citizens are swimming in a sea of toxic pollutants. Many rivers and lakes are unusable even for irrigation; air quality is dangerously unhealthy; and desertification, erosion, and dust storms are depleting arable lands. Public health costs can be measured in early death, chronic disease, lost productivity, and diminished quality of life.

There is little that the developed world can do to help China to implement its environmental laws, which, if enforced, would mitigate some of the worst effects of pollution and even have a secondary benefit of correcting trade imbalances by making Chinese goods more expensive, thereby reducing tensions between China and developed countries. Many of the challenges described in this book are for the Chinese people to solve. However, people in developed countries can engage with China in many other ways, sharing ideas, expertise, and technology and working to change behavior at home so as better to link with the developing world in common cause. This is the urgent challenge for policy makers, ordinary citizens, and readers of this book.

QUESTIONS FOR RESEARCH AND DISCUSSION

1 How should governments deal most fairly with the siting of undesirable but necessary land uses such as garbage dumps, landfills, and polluting factories? How should they ensure that people living near extracted resources enjoy benefits from the extraction?

2 How does China's treatment of minority nationalities compare to such interactions in your own country? Is China's government engaged in a form of environmental injustice, or is it simply using available resources to build the country? How would you improve China's Western Development program to create better options for sustainability and justice?

3 Compare the materials from the International Campaign for Tibet and the Chinese government (links below). How can we explain such radically different views of whether the Tibetans are benefiting from the Han presence?

4 What is the relationship between economic globalization and environmental justice, as reflected in China's trade and investment relationships with other countries? Are the United States and China responsible for monitoring and controlling the ultimate source of products that enter their respective markets?

5 As the West has exported its environmental destruction to China, have China's efforts to protect its environment exported environmental destruction to other countries?

ADDITIONAL RESOURCES

- Basel Action Network: http://www.ban.org/about/ and their report, "Exporting Harm," at http://www.ban.org/E-waste/technotrashfinalcomp.pdf
- China Digital Times map of cancer villages: http://chinadigitaltimes.net/2009/05/a-map-of-chinas-cancer-villages/
- China Tibet Online (government publication): http://eng.tibet.cn/ and Chinese government white paper on Tibet: http://www.china.org.cn/e-white/tibet/index.htm
- Human Rights Watch report on lead poisoning: http://www.hrw.org/reports/2011/06/15/my-children-have-been-poisoned
- International Campaign for Tibet: http://www.savetibet.org/
- "60 Minutes" 2008 story on electronic waste in Guiyu: http://www.cbsnews.com/stories/2008/11/06/60minutes/main4579229.shtml
- Southern Mongolian Human Rights Information Center: http://www.smhric.org/

7 Prospects for the Future ─────────

In only a few generations, China has undergone a transition that now touches every conceivable facet of the country, including the government, the people, civil society, and even intangible cultural characteristics such as identity and tradition. China's rapid economic and much slower political "openings" have drastically changed the landscape, both physically and metaphorically, in ways that could not have been imagined a few decades ago. As we look at present-day China and wonder about the future of its environment, it is easy to be overwhelmed by the enormity of the country's strengths and challenges. How do we begin to draw conclusions? What is the path forward?

From the exposition and analysis in the preceding pages, one fact is clear: China's environment is beset by numerous interconnected and countervailing forces and pressures. This book has attempted to analyze the trends on the ground today, outline the challenges the country faces, and describe where the government and society are facing setbacks or making advances. We have examined the environmental challenges posed by many aspects of China's present situation, including its astronomical growth, the evolving role of the state, and the emergence of civil society. At the same time we have seen that progress toward a sustainable future is hampered by an East-West divide, unequal access to resources, corruption, lax enforcement of regulations, and unresolved and often unacknowledged ethnic conflicts. Even the progress made by middle class and green activists can be illusory if the environmental problems that are tackled in one region are simply exported to another region of China, or another country entirely. These themes intersect and overlap, complement and reinforce, exacerbate and diminish one another in complex ways. To understand one, we need to understand them all.

Consider, for example, the demographic question. Discussion of the country's population size was politically taboo during the Mao years, but since then both government and society have openly acknowledged that it is a powerful constraint on China's development. While debate continues about the growth of the world's most populous nation – including the effect of relaxations of the contentious One Child policy – the sheer number of people and their demands are a powerful force limiting China's choices. At the heart of the country's development is the struggle to bring wealth and comfort to more than one billion people, generations of whom have lived in poverty. One cannot over-state the pressure that this scale of poverty brings on leaders' decision making. Certainly, China has been able to take advantage of globaliza-tion, becoming a manufacturer to the world and expanding its economy drastically. The chances are good that anyone reading this book has something made in China within arm's reach at this very moment. However, with this rising wealth, China's new middle class now demands clean air and water even as its material desires spell trouble for the environment, a contradictory impulse that is not easy for gov-ernment leaders to accommodate.

The primary response of the government to demands for better living standards has been liberalization and decentralization of eco-nomic controls, yet this causes an immense quandary for China's authoritarian state system. Yes, loosening economic restrictions has created conditions for spectacular growth, lifting millions out of poverty. The central government ceded some of its power in a bid to expand the economy; in essence, the state was able to catalyze China's economic turnaround precisely because it had such top-down control to relinquish. However, the "economic miracle" that raised incomes and the national GDP is now also a curse, as the state struggles to limit further destruction of China's natural resources and to begin to clean up the mess generated by decades of environmental abuse. Officials have recognized growing levels of environmental harm – stemming partly from a sense of lawlessness among middle-level officials and industrial leaders – and they have instituted world-class environmental regulations. However, these laws are poorly enforced and the *de facto* reality remains woefully behind the ideal. This implementation gap stems at least in part from a political and social conflict between Western-style economic growth and a healthy environment. For example, deforestation is understood as a problem that creates erosion and flooding at home; the government bans logging in sensitive river headwaters but simultaneously fosters a manufacturing sector that supplies the furniture needs of consumers an ocean away. Thus, the government essentially looks the other way as domestic forests continue to be cut and as timber enters – often illegally – from ravaged forests in Southeast Asia, Russia, and Africa. Water use is a similar arena where the state appears torn between conflicting goals. The massive South-North water transfer is an example: Intended to relieve water shortages in the Northeast, the project has caused dislocation and hardship for local populations and, activists argue, could create environmental problems and increase tensions with surrounding countries whose major rivers will be affected by the plan if the Western route is built. What is more, beyond its borders, China has largely refused to cooperate in regional, transboundary management schemes such as the Mekong River Commission.

The juggernaut that is globalization is the force behind many of China's environmental woes. But globalization can also be a source of hope and a stimulus for innovation. China continues to make strides in developing and producing clean technology; in particular, it invests heavily in areas like solar and wind energy, clean car technology, and desalinization plants, positioning the country to reap profits in the global economy in the future. Perhaps this represents an alternative, realistic path for the future development of China, one where economic and environmental incentives could align. We can see evidence that China is moving in this direction as Chinese civil society groups exercise their new rights to participate in environmental decisions, express their views in the media, and take part in demonstrations, even at times with the blessing of the government. But even as these civil society actors assume a more significant role, their size and effectiveness remain constrained. The Chinese Communist Party remains concerned about unrest that could challenge central authority, and so it closely monitors and controls social movements. Recent history for China has included dark periods of isolation. The openness mandated by a globalized society and modern Internet communication is still viewed with a wary eye, as the government attempts to regulate the flow of ideas while remaining open to the world. The state is in essence performing a high-wire act, balancing the need for centralized control and the suppression of protest against the need for more public participation, more transparency, and greater reliance on the rule of law. A particularly interesting area to monitor for signs of progress in this direction will be the evolving judicial system; its independence will be challenged as civil society begins to test environmental laws and their new rights through the courts. Meanwhile, NGOs must tread carefully, asserting their rights, voicing grievances, and lobbying officials and the media without angering the state so much as to provoke a crackdown.

Emerging civil society also faces questions about its own ability and intent, as it intersects in unusual ways with China's changing demographics and economy. A newly empowered middle class is beginning to demand more of the government with respect to food safety and pollution. The middle-class Chinese environmental movement is growing, as evidenced by the frequency of mass incidents protesting pollution and harmful development. Urban leaders are under intense pressure as community groups and loosely organized citizens confront officials and businesspeople; some measure of justice has been meted out on the corrupt elite. At the same time, these demands also stem from broader popular desires for more consumption and affluence, which promote a lifestyle that contributes to environmental degradation. So, while ENGOs press the government for action, they also need to do some soul searching. Can the environmental movement advocate an alternate path and still draw support from a middle class that at times is focused on material wealth and conspicuous consumption? Successful protests against polluters may shut down a factory, only to cause it to relocate in a more marginal, less powerful community. Severe environmental problems are occurring in ethnic minority communities on the periphery of the country, where a grab for resources is thinly disguised as a development program. In these hinterlands, poor people will increasingly bear the heaviest burden of climate change, yet these communities already suffer racial and class prejudices from the dominant Han. China's burgeoning environmental movement must find a way to balance the desires of its urban support base and wider ideals of environmental justice.

A clear case can be made that the national government – or some parts of it – is inching toward a greater alliance with the green movement, as part of an overall trend toward an expanded civil society and rule by law. Top government officials have recognized that cleaning up the environment requires a combination of stringent legislation, transparent standards and practices, robust institutions, well-defined rights, a democratic process, encouragement of public participation, and engagement with the media. As Qu Geping states in the documentary "Waking the Green Tiger," environmental regulation in any part of the world requires, "supervision from the bottom up." Top-down efforts are important, but some form of green democracy is essential. Additional reforms are needed to encourage such groups and give them more breadth, depth, clout, and legal protections. Western students, activists, organizations, and individuals can find more ways to engage with and support these groups, who have a tough task as they attempt to shift powerful forces toward a different path.

Chinese people have powerful motivations for improving the quality of their lives. The older generation has not forgotten the days of extreme poverty, grueling labor, and sacrifice in the face of famine and death, while younger Chinese are eager to join the world and enjoy their lives. But we can see a cultural complication in China's development and use of its natural resources that stems from the country's national identity and genealogical story of a homogeneous culture that was once the envy of the world. Woven into the cultural fabric of the nation is pride in its former status as the vaunted Middle Kingdom. Neither consumer nor political choices can be divorced from the burden of generations of ingrained insecurity about China's global stature. Today, Chinese strongly desire to reassert status – to gain face, as it were – and finally have the means to do so, having benefited from China's economic transformation and the forces of globalization. Yet this insecurity may also threaten to overheat the economy, overwhelm the environment, and promote ruinous consumption. Incentives to correct course are not readily available when that harm is displaced – to the margins of communities, to rural areas, to the periphery of the country, or outside its borders. We see this preoccupation with face materialized in the predilection for grand construction projects and development. Some of these developments can be understood as legitimate ways to expand a developing economy and alleviate poverty, but others come with tremendous environmental costs. How such tensions are resolved can have grave consequences for the environment and human security, as we have seen in the construction of the controversial Three Gorges Dam and the transfer of water from the Yangzi to the Yellow Rivers. Again, here we wish for an alternative path for China: Can the country pursue prestige and power by leading the way in sustainable development and technology?

A long history of public distrust of central authority also frustrates the government's ability to address challenges. Chinese citizens have a history of circumventing and subverting regulations through bribery. The traditional practice of respecting hierarchies and of seeking relief through the influence of someone more powerful dates back to the time of the emperors. This tendency was exacerbated during the Mao years and during the reforms that followed. During Mao's time, private property and personal wealth were abhorred, and individual citizens had few opportunities to inflict personal damage on the environment. The extensive damage that did occur, as Mao sought to "conquer nature," was directed from the top down. After 1978, when Deng Xiaoping embraced the slogan, "to get rich is glorious," the grip of the state relaxed; but there were few mechanisms to prevent China's venal new entrepreneurs from "looking for money in everything" and exploiting resources and dumping wastes. Regulations, when they were issued, were circumvented. In the old days it was the emperor who lived far away, and was unable to enforce edicts. In the new China, it is the bureaucrats who are distant and ineffectual. Even as law enforcement is gradually given teeth, this dynamic still gives rise to intense pollution of public lands and waterways and high-profile incidents like the 2008 melamine scandal and the 2015 Tianjin chemical explosions. Individuals and small factories are not the only ones to avoid regulation. Even China's largest corporations, like Huaneng and Huadian Power, have been repeatedly fined for failing to obtain environmental permits before constructing dams in the Upper Yangzi watershed.

Asserting the rule of law and creating an ethos where Chinese citizens feel empowered to help preserve and enjoy a clean environment will require enormous effort. Ancient and traditional beliefs and institutions – Confucianism, Daoism, and Buddhism – may provide some guidance. They each speak to the need to promote sustainable relationships, harmony, and respect for the non-human world. But for many young Chinese who find themselves cut off from the past, and who grew up in an intensely materialist and non-religious country, these traditions carry little weight. Fortunately, other traditions can be invoked. Environmental groups emphasize a love of nature for its own sake, encouraging nature walks, photography, tree planting, and preservation of wild lands, rivers, and animals. The scientific evidence for the causes of our environmental crisis speaks loudly in a country that values education, technical solutions, and economic prosperity. Social justice, distributive justice, the rights of individuals and minorities, and the desire to project China as a leading and positive force in the world are also powerful sentiments that underpin communist ideology and form a patriotic identity. If these new convictions and older traditions are combined, could they prevail in the face of corruption, materialism, and a central government deeply suspicious of political and social movements? Some activists and even officials suggest that it is possible and inevitable, because the alternative is unsustainable.

Finally, we must consider the complex challenge posed by the East-West divide. Vast areas of western China, home to rural peasants and ethnic minorities, remain relatively untouched by the modernization and growing wealth of the East, despite the government push to create new urban metropolises that will stimulate the largely untapped consumer market there and fuel China's economic growth. The China of Beijing or Shanghai is a vastly different place from Tibet, Xinjiang, or Inner Mongolia or even the rural farming areas of the country. In these areas, life has changed little overall and in some places basic needs remain unsatisfied. Residents remain excluded from much of China's development, disconnected from the country's gleaming cities and rise to prominence. The sheer numbers of poor give impetus to the state's growth and development targets. But the poor tend to benefit least, as wealth trickles too slowly from the urban megalopolis to the rural village, and income inequalities worsen with every passing year. When we take a closer look at these regions, we suspect that government attempts to "develop" infrastructure are often no more than strategies to extract natural resources at the expense of a marginalized population. Development campaigns, and even some environmental campaigns like the restoration of the grasslands discussed earlier, may also result in the dislocation of minorities or enforced assimilation as entire communities are broken up. Meanwhile, as pollution protests in the wealthy East grow stronger, much environmental harm is simply displaced to the periphery. In some cases, this practice undermines the government's legitimacy and fuels ongoing struggles that threaten China's stability.

Although the evidence presented in this book does not suggest that China has reached a point of no return in terms of environmental degradation, taken together, the environmental challenges suggest that China, its government, and its people will have to grapple with a long list of questions as they attempt to build what they call a harmonious and sustainable society:

- What is the ultimate goal of China's economic development model? Can the country afford a trajectory modeled on that of the West? Can the rest of the world afford it?
- Where does the state fit into the picture of environmental governance? Does the state have the political will or ability to eschew a growth-at-all-costs mentality?
- What is the path ahead for China's home grown, if nascent, environmental movement? Can it be inclusive without compromising values? Who does it ultimately represent? Can it challenge the government and business interests effectively? Can it form and maintain useful relationships with the international environmental movement?
- Can the Chinese people search their souls during their quest for an improved quality of life? Can they avoid the excesses of the Global North that displaced so much environmental harm onto the developing South? Can they collectively choose an alternative develop-

ment model that might rest on post-materialist values emphasizing fulfillment and the construction of a meaningful life rather than material consumption?

- Is China's model addressing broad issues of injustice and oppression of poor and minority voices? Or is this economic model only contributing to further exploitation of those who live at the margins and beyond China's borders? What would greater inclusion mean for China and its people?

- Where does the international community fit in? Where does China fit into the international community? If the environment is truly a global issue, does the world not have a responsibility to China and vice versa? What lessons does China have to offer the rest of the world? If China is greening itself, is it doing so at the cost of vulnerable populations elsewhere?

Answers to these questions will not come easily. Complex challenges within China overlap and intersect in ways that rule out quick fixes. And while there are clear reasons for hope, time is running short. As we have seen in the preceding chapters, the choices China is facing are extremely difficult. There is huge pressure for China to continue on its current path of rapid growth coupled with environmental degradation, both within and beyond borders. The ability to shift course is constrained by historical and cultural baggage that puts the emphasis on global recognition and conspicuous consumption.

There are encouraging signs that a shift is under way, with greater confidence in the legal system, increased public participation and information transparency, and broad recognition that development that chokes and harms is undesirable. Significant forces are working tirelessly for greater attention to and emphasis on sustainability, including within the Chinese state system. As we have seen, China and the world are so intertwined that what happens in China not only impacts all of us, but what all of us do has an impact in China. Through our buying habits, political action in our home countries, information sharing, and other choices that we make every day, we can join with those in China working for a sustainable future. Yet if China's policy makers, corporations, and politically powerful middle class, along with other global actors and each one of us through our individual decisions, continue to displace harms onto yet more vulnerable populations and future generations, then joined together as we are as a planet, we will continue to accumulate debt that can never be repaid.

FINAL THOUGHTS

Here are a few reflections with which to conclude this investigation of China's environmental challenges. Today, we know much more than we did even 30 years ago about the dynamics of the global ecosystems that sustain us. Wherever we live, we are connected to China, and to each other. We share air, water, food, oceans, wildlife, agricultural harvests, and toxic wastes. We are dependent on each other for the food, shelter, and the material objects that make our lives more comfortable and interesting. We have learned, slowly, to recognize the priceless and invisible services that our ecosystems provide, from water purification to carbon fixation to pollination. We understand the importance of the variety of life species, from charismatic megafauna like Siberian tigers and pandas to the humble and tiny sea creatures that build the reefs that nurture the fish that feed us. With and without religion, we have been able to find inspiration and renewal in the natural world. As communities, we find meaning in our greater understanding of the capacity of all creatures, human and non-human, to communicate and to seek lives free from suffering. Yet we also urgently mourn our losses: the disappearance each day of the last surviving member of a species, the rapidly melting polar ice sheets and sea-level rise even more dramatic than first feared, the noticeably more frequent severe weather events such as droughts and cyclones.

We feel deeply uneasy at the apparent inadequacy of the state system to deal with global and transboundary challenges such as climate change or the illegal trade in endangered species. Where treaties have been signed and ratified, weak implementation and enforcement suggest that the agreements are unequal to the magnitude of the challenges we face. We understand that the predictable and progressive collapse of ecosystems and degradation of the global environment within the lifetimes of those already born are linked to the inability of national governments to act, to an exploding human population, and to a relentless economic globalization that unleashes forces difficult to control. The world's thirst for limited natural resources like fossil fuels, minerals, timber, and fish has sparked fierce international competition and new sources of conflict. This is the "resource curse" that sometimes turns developing nations into battlefields for external powers and multinational businesses competing for access to the materials to feed economic growth and profits, often at the expense of local populations and the environment.

We recognize that there is something profoundly wrong with the way we are doing business as a planet. We need to reject the drive for economic growth at all costs and establish a different concept of security – human, state, and global – that is linked to respect for the limitations of the planet's non-renewable resources. As the United Nations Environment Programme argues, we must "decouple" the planet's quest for prosperity from its unsustainable use of resources (Fischer-Kowalski and Swilling 2011). We must also understand that the "ecological footprint" of a nation can be correctly measured only by considering international as well as domestic extraction of resources; so too with the disposal of pollution and toxic waste. All environmental problems are ultimately globally shared – we can neither export them nor build a protective wall to keep them out. We need to create the political space to allow countries like China to perform better, to satisfy them that developed countries are doing their fair share to deal with the problems for which industrial societies are primarily responsible. At the same time, the world needs to do more to help developing countries to curb some of the worst impacts of the pollution and climate change that will ultimately be felt most sharply among the world's poor. In international environmental law, this concept is enshrined in the principle of "common but differentiated responsibilities," which acknowledges that we have a shared interest in dealing with the globe's enormous environmental challenges, but that the developed world needs to go first to resolve the problems. It also needs to help the developing world to pay for its transformation to a cleaner, more sustainable development model. The "right to development" is also a powerful principle of international environmental law, and the globe must find ways to respect this. China could, indeed it must, be a modern laboratory for designing a new path. As we have seen, China holds a special place on the world environmental stage. In so many ways, China's route to the future will be that of the planet.

China observers these days often fall into two camps: critics and apologists. Yet this book has called for a more nuanced response. Outsiders dealing with China must see the whole picture, good and bad, and think strategically about how to boost the promise and minimize the peril. The concepts around which this book has been organized may help readers in the developed world to reflect on how we can support China in this effort. As for Chinese readers of this book, I hope that a perspective that draws on the concepts and perspectives from the outside world may be useful for building alliances and considering China's enormous environmental challenges afresh.

In terms of governance, we can support the actors within the central government who are trying to "green" the country's administrative patterns by acknowledging and praising them in international forums, providing and welcoming international expertise to help them craft win-win solutions that will gain wide acceptance by the laggards within the bureaucracy, and strengthen their efforts to spread rule of law by continuing the academic and governmental exchanges that have already borne so much fruit. We can remove obstacles to the transfer and dissemination of clean technology and create strong international mechanisms to help China, and the rest of the developing world, avoid exacerbating the global environmental crisis for which we in the developed world are largely responsible. In terms of national identity, we can engage in the discussion by sharing resources about other nations' struggles with these questions, including Chinese scholars in debates about culture and sustainability, and encouraging and facilitating publication in Chinese of relevant books and documents. We can try to foster a sense that an international community is together searching for ways to shift human culture from one of exploitation of nature to one of respect and care. In terms of civil society, Chinese citizens' groups can benefit from opportunities for their leaders to travel overseas to network with their peers, attend international negotiations, study abroad, and obtain resources to fund their activities. We can also support those who have been subjected to political repression by raising their names in international forums and encouraging the Chinese government to permit more space for free expression and public participation. Finally, in terms of equity and the displacement of harm, we can all become more sensitive to problems of environmental justice across time, space, and species, by considering the impacts of global consumption patterns on resource extraction and waste disposal, and understanding more clearly how the negative externalities of these activities tend to harm the most vulnerable, both human and non-human. While awareness of the ethical dimensions of our behavior will not in itself shift us away from destructive patterns, it may bring to light what has been hidden and make it more difficult to pursue the old ways.

True security will come not from foreign wars or expansion of overseas influence in an effort to secure the last few generations' worth of the earth's treasures. Rather, it will come from tapping energy and using products derived close to home, through the wide-scale adoption of renewable technologies and reusable materials. In national planning, all countries must strive to move toward what ecological economist Herman Daly (1996) has called a "steady-state economy," while making allowances for countries that cannot yet do so; in production, they must move toward what architect William McDonough and chemist Michael Braungart (2002) call "cradle-to-cradle" lifecycles, such that once taken from the earth, resources can be used over and over again, forever.

Making this transition will take tremendous political will and effort. It will require leadership from China, the U.S., and Europe, from developed and developing countries, from the Global North and the Global South. It must come from each individual, from each community, from each province, and from each nation. The goal is development that truly benefits all citizens, with healthy air and water, rich forests and jungles that are home to a biodiversity of animals, plants, birds, and insects, urban parks where citizens can reconnect to nature, and human lives whose meanings are measured not by material consumption or possessions but by compassion, connection to others, and reverence for life.

References ──────────────────────────

Anderson, Benedict (1983) *Imagined Communities: Reflections on the Origin and Spread of Nationalism.* London: Verso.

Avedon, John (1984) *In Exile from the Land of Snows: The Definitive Account of the Dalai Lama and Tibet since the Chinese Conquest.* New York: Knopf.

Bai, Xuemei (2008) The urban transition in China: Trends, consequences and policy implications. In: Martine, George; McGranahan, Gordon; Montgomery, Mark; and Fernández-Castilla, Rogelio (eds), *The New Global Frontier: Urbanization, Poverty and Environment in the 21st Century.* London: Routledge.

Balk, Deborah; McGranahan, Gordon; and Anderson, Bridget (2007) Rising tide: Assessing the risks of climate change and human settlements in low elevation coastal zones. *Environment & Urbanization,* 19(1): 17–37.

Bauer, Joanne (ed.) (2006) *Forging Environmentalism: Justice, Livelihood and Contested Environments.* Armonk, NY: M.E. Sharpe.

Becker, Jasper (1997) *Hungry Ghosts: Mao's Secret Famine.* New York: Free Press.

Bi, Jiajing (2011) China's "green aid" offers lessons for the world. *Revolt: The Worldwatch Institute's Climate and Energy Blog.* [online] April 29, 2011. Available at: http://blogs.worldwatch.org/revolt/chinas-"green-aid" -offers-lessons-for-the-world/ (accessed March 20, 2015).

Bittman, Mark (2013) On becoming China's farm team. *The New York Times.* November 5, 2013.

Blaikie, Piers (1985) *Political Economy of Soil Erosion in Developing Countries.* London: Longman.

Blomeyer, Roland; Goulding, Ian; Pauly, Daniel; Sanz, Antonio and Stobberup, Kim (2012) *Role of China in World Fisheries.* The European Parliament, Directorate General Internal Policies, Policy Department B Structural and Cohesion Policies – Fisheries. Brussels.

Bongiorni, Sarah (2007) *A Year without "Made in China."* New York: John Wiley & Sons.

Bookchin, Murray (1980) *Toward an Ecological Society.* Montreal: Black Rose Books.

BP Statistical Review of World Energy (2014) [online]. Available at: http://www.bp.com/content/dam/bp/pdf/Energy-economics/statistical -review-2014/BP-statistical-review-of-world-energy-2014-full-report.pdf (accessed June 1, 2015).

Bradsher, Keith (2009) China's incinerators loom as global hazard. *The New York Times*. August 11, 2009.

Brandon, John J. (2011) Water: quenching the thirst for security? *In Asia.* [online] June 22, 2011. Available at http://asiafoundation.org/in-asia/2011/06/22/ water-quenching-the-thirst-for-security (accessed March 20, 2015).

Brautigam, Deborah (2009) *The Dragon's Gift: The Real Story of China in Africa*. New York: Oxford University Press.

Brettell, Anna (2008) Channeling dissent: the institutionalization of environmental complaint resolution in China. In: Ho, Peter and Edmonds, Richard L. (eds). *China's Embedded Activism: Opportunities and Constraints of a Social Movement*. London: Routledge.

Brown, Lester (1995) *Who Will Feed China? Wake-Up Call for a Small Planet*. New York: W.W. Norton & Co.

Bruun, Ole and Kalland, Arne (1995) *Asian Perceptions of Nature: A Critical Approach*. London: Routledge.

Central European University Center for Environmental Policy and Law (2007) *Making the Case for Environmental Justice in Central and Eastern Europe*. Budapest: Central European University. Available at: http://www.env-health .org/IMG/pdf/28-_Making_the_case_for_environmental_justice_in _Europe.pdf (accessed July 31, 2015).

Chellaney, Brahma (2013) *Water: Asia's New Battleground*. Washington, DC: Georgetown University Press.

China Daily (2011) China to ease NGO registration policy. *China Daily*. July 11, 2011.

China Radio International (2011) New garbage incinerator planned in Haidian. *CRI English*. [online] January 20, 2011. Available at: http://english.cri. cn/6909/2011/01/20/2743s616531.htm (accessed March 20, 2015).

Dai, Qing (1994) *Yangtze! Yangtze!* Adams, Patricia and Thibodeau, John (eds); translated from the Chinese by Nancy Liu. London, Toronto: Earthscan.

Dai, Qing (1998) *The River Dragon Has Come! The Three Gorges Dam and the Fate of China's Yangtze River and Its People*. Thibodeau, John and Williams, Philip (eds); translated from the Chinese by Yi Ming. Armonk, NY: M.E. Sharpe.

Dalai Lama XIV (1990) *Freedom in Exile*. London: Hodder and Stoughton.

Daly, Herman (1996) *Beyond Growth: The Economics of Sustainable Development*. Boston, MA: Beacon Press.

Dauvergne, Peter (1997) *Shadows in the Forest: Japan and the Politics of Timber in Southeast Asia.* Cambridge, MA: MIT Press.

Diamond, Larry (2009) *The Spirit of Democracy: The Struggle to Build Free Societies Throughout the World.* New York: Times Books.

Dikötter, Frank (2010) *Mao's Great Famine: The History of China's Most Devastating Catastrophe, 1958–1962.* New York: Walker and Company.

Dittmer, Lowell and Yu, George T. (eds) (2010) *China, the Developing World and the New Global Dynamic.* London: Lynne Rienner Publishers.

Economy, Elizabeth C. (2004) *River Runs Black: The Environmental Challenge to China's Future.* Ithaca, NY: Cornell University Press.

Economy, Elizabeth C. and Levi, Michael (2014) *By All Means Necessary: How China's Resource Quest is Changing the World.* New York: Oxford University Press.

Ehrlich, Paul and Holdren, John T. (1971) Impact of population growth. *Science,* 171(3977): 1212–17.

Evasdottir, Erika (2004) *Obedient Autonomy: Chinese Intellectuals and the Achievement of Orderly Life.* Vancouver: University of British Columbia Press.

Fairley, Peter (2009) China's potent wind potential: Forecasters see no need for new coal and nuclear power plants. *Technology Review.* [online] September 14, 2009. Available at: http://www.technologyreview.com/energy/23460/?a-f (accessed March 20, 2015).

Fischer-Kowalski, Marina and Swilling, Mark (2011) *Decoupling: Natural Resource Use and Environmental Impacts from Economic Growth.* New York: United Nations Environment Programme.

Forbes (2014) *The World's Billionaires.* [online]. Available at: http://www.forbes.com/billionaires/list (accessed March 20, 2015).

Fortune, CNN and Money (2014) *Global 500.* [online]. Available at: http://fortune.com/global500/ (accessed March 20, 2015).

Freeman, Carla (2011) *Quenching the Dragon's Thirst.* Washington, DC: Woodrow Wilson Center.

French, Howard W. (2014) *China's Second Continent: How a Million Migrants Are Building a New Empire in Africa.* New York: Alfred A. Knopf.

Friends of Nature and Chinese Academy of Social Sciences (2007–2011, multiple volumes), *China Environment Yearbook.* Leiden: Brill.

Friends of Nature, Institute of Public & Environmental Affairs, Green Beagle, Envirofriends and Green Stone Environmental Action Network (2011) *The Other Side of Apple II: Pollution Spreads through Apple's Supply Chain.* [online]. Available at: http://www.ipe.org.cn/Upload/Report-IT-V-Apple-II.pdf (accessed March 20, 2015).

Fu, Jing (2010) Urban-rural income gap widest since reform. *China Daily*. March 2, 2010.

Gao, Qingzhu; Li, Yu'e; Wan, Yunfan; Lin, Erda; Xiong, Wei; Jiangcun, Wangzha; Wang, Baoshan; and Li, Wenfu (2006) Grassland degradation in Northern Tibet based on remote sensing data. *Journal of Geographical Sciences*, 16(2): 165–73.

Geall, Sam (ed.) (2013) *China and the Environment: The Green Revolution*. London: Zed Books.

Geertz, Clifford (1973) *Interpretation of Cultures*. New York: Basic Books.

Goodman, Peter and Finn, Peter (2007) Corruption stains timber trade. *Washington Post*. April 1, 2007.

Gramsci, Antonio (1991) *Prison Notebooks*. New York: Columbia University Press.

Gries, Peter Hays (2005) *China's New Nationalism: Pride, Politics, and Diplomacy*. Berkeley, CA: University of California Press.

Harrell, Stevan (ed.) (1995) *Cultural Encounters on China's Ethnic Frontiers*. Seattle, WA: University of Washington Press.

Harris, Richard (2010) Rangeland degradation on the Qinghai-Tibetan plateau: A review of the evidence of its magnitude and causes. *Journal of Arid Environments*, 74(1): 1–12.

Hessel, Dieter T. and Ruether, Rosemary Radford (eds) (2000) *Christianity and Ecology: Seeking the Well-Being of Earth and Humans*. Cambridge, MA: Harvard University Center for the Study of World Religions.

Human Rights Watch (2011a) *My Children Have Been Poisoned: A Public Health Crisis in Four Chinese Provinces*. New York: Human Rights Watch.

Human Rights Watch (2011b) *You'll Be Fired if You Refuse: Labor Abuses in Chinese State-owned Copper Mines*. New York: Human Rights Watch.

Immerzeel, Walter W.; van Beek, Ludovicus P.H.; and Bierkens, Marc F.P. (2010) Climate change will affect the Asian Water Towers. *Science*, 328(5984): 1382–85.

International Rivers Network (n.d.) *South-North Water Transfer Project*. [online]. Available at: http://www.internationalrivers.org/en/china/south-north-water-transfer-project (accessed March 20, 2015).

Jacobs, Andrew (2011) The privileges of China's elite include purified air. *The New York Times*. November 4, 2011.

Jahiel, Abigail (1997) Contradictory impact of reform on environmental protection in China. *China Quarterly*, 149: 83–103.

Jahiel, Abigail (1998) Organization of environmental protection in China. *China Quarterly*, 156: 757–87.

Jansson, Johanna (2013) Sicomines agreement revisited: Prudent Chinese banks and risk-taking Chinese companies. *Review of African Political Economy*, 40(135): 152–62.

Jiang, Rong (2008) *Wolf Totem*. Translated from the Chinese by Howard Goldblatt. New York: Penguin Press.

Johnson, Ian (2011) Train wreck in China heightens unease on safety standards. *The New York Times*. July 24, 2011.

Johnson, Todd M.; Liu, Feng; and Newfarmer, Richard (1997) *Clear Water, Blue Skies: China's Environment in the New Century*. Washington, DC: World Bank.

Kahn, Joseph and Yardley, Jim (2007) Choking on growth: A series of articles and multimedia examining China's pollution crisis. *The New York Times*. Multiple dates.

Keck, Margaret E. and Sikkink, Kathryn (1998) *Activists beyond Borders: Advocacy Networks in International Politics*. Ithaca, NY: Cornell University Press.

Kjøllesdal, Kristian and Welle-Strand, Anne (2010) Foreign aid strategies: China taking over? *Asian Social Science*, 6(10): 3–13.

Klugman, Jeni (2011) *Human Development Report 2011 Sustainability and Equity: A Better Future for All*. New York: United Nations Development Programme.

Kolbert, Elizabeth (2014) *Sixth Extinction: An Unnatural History*. New York: Henry Holt.

Krishnan, Ananth (2011) An enlightened hue to protests in China. *The Hindu*. August 16, 2011.

LaFraniere, Sharon (2011) Lead poisoning in China: The hidden scourge. *The New York Times*. June 15, 2011.

Lam, Cory (2011) 12th five year plan hailed as "greenest FYP in China's history." *China Briefing*. [online] April 12, 2011. Available at http://www.china-briefing.com/news/2011/04/05/12th-five-year-plan-hailed-as-greenest-fyp-in-chinas-history.html (accessed March 20, 2015).

Li, Jing (2011) Green industries to add millions of jobs. *China Daily*. November 16, 2011.

Liang, Heng and Shapiro, Judith (1983) *Son of the Revolution*. New York: Alfred A. Knopf.

Lieberthal, Kenneth (2003) *Governing China: From Revolution through Reform*, 2nd ed. New York: W.W. Norton.

Link, Perry (1992) *Evening Chats in Beijing: Probing China's Predicament*. New York: Norton.

Liu, Binyan (1990) *A Higher Kind of Loyalty: A Memoir by China's Foremost Journalist.* New York: Pantheon Books.

Liu, Lee (2010) Made in China: Cancer villages. *Environment: Science and Policy for Sustainable Development,* 52(2): 8–21.

Loh, Christine (2011) Contrasting realities: China's environmental challenge. *China Rights Forum No. 1 & 2 – China at a Crossroads.* New York: Human Rights in China.

Lora-Wainwright, Anna (2014) *Fighting for Breath: Living Morally and Dying of Cancer in a Chinese Village.* Honolulu, HI: University of Hawaii Press.

Lowe, Justin (1992) Scorched earth: China's assault on Tibet's environment. *Multinational Monitor,* 13(10): 15–19.

Lü, Zhi and Turner, Jennifer (2006) Building a green civil society in China. In: *State of the World 2006.* New York: W.W. Norton.

Lum, Thomas; Fischer, Hannah; Gomez-Granger, Julissa; and Leland, Anne (2009) *China's Foreign Aid Activities in Africa, Latin America and Southeast Asia.* Congressional Research Service. [online]. Available at: http://www.fas.org/sgp/crs/row/R40361.pdf (accessed March 20, 2015).

Ma, Bo (1996) *Blood Red Sunset: A Memoir of the Chinese Cultural Revolution.* Translated from the Chinese by Howard Goldblatt. London: Penguin.

Ma, Jun (2004) *China's Water Crisis.* Norwalk, CT: Eastbridge.

Ma, Tianjie (2008/2009) Environmental mass incidents in rural China: Examining large-scale unrest in Dongyang, Zhejiang. *China Environment Series,* 10: 33–56. Washington, DC: Woodrow Wilson Center.

Ma, Tianjie (2015) Put China's tough new law to protect the environment to the test. *South China Morning Post.* January 14, 2015.

Ma, Xiaoying and Ortolano, Leonard (2000) *Environmental Regulation in China: Institutions, Enforcement, and Compliance.* Oxford: Rowman and Littlefield.

Mallory, T.G. (2013) China's distant water fishing industry: Evolving policies and implications. *Marine Policy,* 38: 99–108.

Marcuse, Gary, director (2011) *Waking the Green Tiger* [film]. Vancouver: Face to Face Media.

Marcuse, Gary, director (2014) *Searching for Sacred Mountain* [film]. Vancouver: Face to Face Media.

Marks, Robert (2006) *Tigers, Rice, Silk, and Silt: Environment and Economy in Late Imperial South China.* Cambridge: Cambridge University Press.

Marston, Rebecca (2011) No rules for the rich: How China spends its new wealth. *BBC.* [online] May 11, 2011. Available at: http://www.bbc.co.uk/news/business-13284481 (accessed March 20, 2015).

Mastny, Lisa (ed.) (2010) *Renewable Energy and Energy Efficiency in China: Current Status and Prospects for 2020*. Washington, DC: Worldwatch Institute.

Matthiessen, Peter (1978) *The Snow Leopard*. New York: Viking.

McDonough, William and Braungart, Michael (2002) *Cradle To Cradle: Remaking The Way We Make Things*. New York: North Point Press.

McElwee, Charles R. (2011) *Environmental Law in China: Managing Risk and Ensuring Compliance*. Oxford: Oxford University Press.

Mertha, Andrew (2008) *China's Water Warriors: Citizen Action and Policy Change*. Ithaca, NY: Cornell University Press.

Ministry of Commerce, People's Republic of China (2014) Statistics of FDI from January to September 2014, http://english.mofcom.gov.cn/article/statistic/foreigninvestment/201411/20141100814297.shtml (accessed January 15, 2015).

Ministry of Environmental Protection, People's Republic of China (2014). *Annual Report on the State of the Environment in China in 2013*. Beijing [online] Available at: http://jcs.mep.gov.cn/hjzl/zkgb/2013zkgb/ (accessed January 26, 2015).

Minx, Jan C.; Baiocchi, Giovanni; Peters, Glen P.; Weber, Christopher L.; Guan, Dabo; and Hubacek, Klaus (2011) A "carbonizing dragon": China's fast growing CO_2 emissions revisited. *Environmental Science and Technology*, 45(21): 9144–53.

Mittelman, James H. (2000) *Globalization Syndrome*. Princeton, NJ: Princeton University Press.

Moore, Malcolm (2008) "China Plans Dams across Tibet." *The Telegraph*. October 14.

Morton, Katherine (2005) *International Aid and China's Environment*. London: Taylor & Francis.

Needham, Joseph (multiple dates, 27 volumes) *Science and Civilization in China*. Cambridge: Cambridge University Press.

Neuman, William (2014) Vegetable spawns larceny and luxury in Peru. *New York Times*. December 6, 2014.

OECD (2007) *OECD Environmental Performance Review of China*. Paris: Organization for Economic Cooperation and Development.

Osnos, Evan (2014) *Age of Ambition: Chasing Fortune, Truth, and Faith in the New China*. New York: Farrar, Straus & Giroux.

Pai, Hsiao-Hung (2012) Chinese rural migrant workers deserve more respect from the city-dwellers. *The Guardian*. August 25, 2012.

Painter, Michael and Durham, William H. (eds) (1995) *Social Causes of Environmental Destruction in Latin America*. Ann Arbor, MI: University of Michigan Press.

Pan, Jiahua; Ma, Haibing; and Zhang, Ying (2011) *Green Economy and Green Jobs in China: Current Status and Potentials for 2020.* Washington, DC: Worldwatch Institute.

Pierson, David (2011) Coal mining in China's Inner Mongolia fuels tensions. *The Los Angeles Times.* June 2, 2011.

Qu, Geping and Li, Jinchang (1994) *Population and the Environment in China [Zhongguo renkou yu Huanjing].* Boulder, CO: Lynne Rienner.

Ramzy, Austin (2014) China's solar panel production comes at a dirty cost. *The New York Times.* June 2, 2014.

Sanderson, Henry and Forsythe, Michael (2013) *China's Superbank: Debt, Oil and Influence – How China Development Bank Is Rewriting the Rules of Finance.* New York: Bloomberg Press.

Schaller, George (1993) *The Last Panda.* Chicago, IL: University of Chicago Press.

Schmalzer, Sigrid (2008) *The People's Peking Man: Popular Science and Human Identity in Twentieth-Century China.* Chicago, IL: University of Chicago Press.

Scott, James C. (1985) *Weapons of the Weak: Everyday Forms of Peasant Resistance.* New Haven, CT: Yale University Press.

Scott, James C. (1998) *Seeing Like a State: How Certain Schemes to Improve the Human Condition Have Failed.* New Haven, CT: Yale University Press.

Shalizi, Zmarak (2006) *Addressing China's Growing Water Shortages and Associated Social and Environmental Consequences.* Washington, DC: World Bank.

Shapiro, Judith (2001) *Mao's War against Nature: Politics and the Environment in Revolutionary China.* Cambridge: Cambridge University Press.

Shifflett, Susan Chan (2015) China's Hottest Tech Giants Join the "War on Pollution". [online] January 31. Available at: http://www.wilsoncenter.org/article/chinas-hottest-tech-giants-join-the-war-pollution (accessed June 6, 2015).

Simons, Craig (2013) *The Devouring Dragon: How China's Rise Threatens Our Natural World.* New York: St. Martin's.

Sinkule, Barbara J. and Ortolano, Leonard (1995) *Implementing Environmental Policy in China.* Westport, CT: Praeger.

Smith, David (2013) Chinese appetite for shark fin soup devastating Mozambique coastline. *The Guardian.* February 14, 2013.

Stalley, Phillip (2010) *Foreign Firms, Investment, and Environmental Regulation in the People's Republic of China.* Stanford, CA: Stanford University Press.

Stern, David (2003) Environmental Kuznets curve. *Internet Encyclopedia of Ecological Economics.* [online]. Available at: http://www.ecoeco.org/pdf/stern .pdf (accessed January 7, 2012).

Su, Xiaokang (1988) River Elegy. [film series] China.

Sun, Xiufang and Canby, Kerstin (2010) *China: Overview of Forest Governance, Markets and Trade.* Washington, DC: Forest Trends.

Sze, Julie (2015) *Fantasy Islands: Chinese Dreams and Ecological Fears in an Age of Climate Crisis.* Berkeley, CA: University of California.

Teets, Jessica (2014) *Civil Society under Authoritarianism: The China Model.* Cambridge: Cambridge University Press.

Thubron, Colin (1989) *Behind the Wall: A Journey through China.* New York: Atlantic Monthly Press.

Thubron, Colin (2007) *Shadow of the Silk Road.* London: Chatto & Windus.

United Nations Office of the High Commissioner for Human Rights (UNOHCHR) (2012) *Report of the Special Rapporteur on the right to food. Olivier De Schutter: Mission to China.* http://www2.ohchr.org/english/bodies/hrcouncil/docs/19session/A.HRC.19.59.Add.1.pdf (accessed January 20, 2015).

U.S. Department of State (2013) *Report of the Visa Office.* Bureau of Consular Services. [online]. http://travel.state.gov/content/visas/english/law-and-policy/statistics/annual-reports/report-of-the-visa-office-2013.html (accessed January 16, 2015).

U.S. Department of the Treasury (2014) *Major Foreign Holders of Treasury Securities.* [online]. Available at: http://www.treasury.gov/resource-center/data-chart-center/tic/Documents/mfh.txt (accessed January 15, 2015).

Vanacore, Tara Sun (2012) *Snapshot: China's Waste Challenge.* China Environment Forum. Washington, DC: Woodrow Wilson International Center for Scholars [online]. Available at: http://www.wilsoncenter.org/publication/snapshot-chinas-waste-challenge (accessed April 3, 2015).

Vermont Law School (2010) *U.S.-Asia Partnerships for Environmental Law.* [online]. Available at: http://www.vermontlaw.edu/academics/centers-and-programs/us-asia (accessed March 20, 2015).

Voice of America (2011) Chinese VP pledges accelerated development in Tibet. [online] July 19, 2011. Available at: http://www.voanews.com/tibetan-english/news/Chinese-VP-Pledges-Accelerated-Development-in-Tibet-125805533.html (accessed March 20, 2015).

Wallerstein, Immanuel (1979) *Capitalist World-Economy.* Cambridge: Cambridge University Press.

Wang, Xiaoyi (2007) *Undermining Grassland Management through Centralized Environmental Policies in Inner Mongolia.* Washington, DC: World Resources Institute.

Wapner, Paul (1995) Politics beyond the state: Environmental activism and world civic politics. *World Politics,* 47(3): 311–40.

Watts, Jonathan (2010a) China's "cancer villages" reveal dark side of economic boom. *The Guardian*. June 6, 2010.

Watts, Jonathan (2010b) *When a Billion Chinese Jump: How China Will Save Mankind – Or Destroy It*. New York: Simon & Schuster.

Watts, Jonathan (2011) China's love affair with the car shuns green vehicles. *The Guardian*. August 24, 2011.

Wee, Sui-Lee (2011) China says will shut plant as thousands protest. *Reuters*. August 14, 2011.

Wee, Sui-Lee (2015) In China, a fight to save a forest tests toughened environment law. *Reuters*. February 10, 2015.

Weller, Robert P. (2006) *Discovering Nature: Globalization and Environmental Culture in China and Taiwan*. Cambridge: Cambridge University Press.

White Jr., Lynn T. (1967) The historical roots of our ecological crisis. *Science*, 155(3767): 1203–7.

Willer, Helga and Lernoud, Julia (2014) *Organic Agriculture Worldwide: Current Statistics*. [online]. Available at: http://www.fibl.org/fileadmin/documents/de/news/2014/willer-2014-global-data.pdf (accessed March 20, 2015).

Wines, Michael (2011) Bystanders' neglect of injured toddler sets off soul-searching on web sites in China. *New York Times*. October 18, 2011.

Wines, Michael and Ansfield, Jonathan (2010) Trampled in a land rush, Chinese resist. *New York Times*. May 26, 2010.

Wittfogel, Karl (1957) *Oriental Despotism: A Comparative Study of Total Power*. New Haven, CT: Yale University Press.

Woetzel, Jonathan; Mendonca, Lenny; Devan, Janamitra; Negri, Stefano; Hu, Yamgei; Jordan, Luke; Li, Xiujun; Maasry, Alexander; Tsen, Geoff; and Yu, Flora (2009) *Preparing for China's Urban Billion*. McKinsey Global Institute. [online]. Available at: http://www.mckinsey.com/Insights/MGI/Research/Urbanization/Preparing_for_urban_billion_in_China (accessed March 20, 2015).

World Commission on Environment and Development (WCED) (1987) *Our Common Future*. Oxford: Oxford University Press.

World Nuclear Association (2013) *Nuclear Power in China*. [online]. Available at: http://www.world-nuclear.org/info/inf63.html (accessed March 20, 2015).

World Resources Institute (1999) *China's Health and Environment: Air Pollution and Health Effects*. Washington, DC: World Resources Institute.

World Trade Organization (WTO) (2014) *China Trade Profile*. [online]. Available at: http://stat.wto.org/CountryProfile/WSDBCountryPFView.aspx?Language=E&Country=CN (accessed March 20, 2015).

Wu, Fengshi (2002) New partners or old brothers? GONGOs in transnational environmental advocacy in China. *China Environment Series*, 5: 47–53.

Wu, Wencong (2011) E-waste still fuels pollution, says NGO. *China Daily*. May 9, 2011.

Xie, Jian (2009) *Addressing China's Water Scarcity: Recommendations for Selected Water Resource Management Issues*. Washington, DC: World Bank.

Xie, Xiaoping (2011) Apple breaks its silence. *China Dialogue*. [online] October 3, 2011. Available at: http://www.chinadialogue.net/article/show/single/en/4561 (accessed March 20, 2015).

Xinhua (2015) 76 percent of China's luxury consumption happens overseas: report. Xinhua News Agency. January 31, 2015.

Yan, Yunxiang (2013) Food safety and social risk in contemporary China. In: Link, Perry; Madsen, Richard P. and Pickowicz, Paul (eds), *Restless China*. Lanham, MD: Rowman & Littlefield.

Yang, Ruby, director (2010) *Warriors of Qiugang* [film]. Beijing: Thomas Lennon Films & Chang Ai Media Project.

Yeh, Emily (2009) Greening western China: A critical view. *Geoforum*, 40(5): 884–94.

Yeh, Emily (2014) *Taming Tibet: Landscape Transformation and the Gift of Chinese Development*. Ithaca, NY: Cornell University Press.

Yu, LiAnne (2014) *Consumption in China: How China's New Consumer Ideology Is Shaping the Nation*. Cambridge: Polity.

Zhang, Bo and Cao, Cong (2015) Policy: Four gaps in China's new environmental law. *Nature*, 517(753): 433–4.

Zhao, Michael (2015) Why has this environmental documentary gone viral on China's Internet? *ChinaFile*. [online] March 3, 2015. Available at: http://www.chinafile.com/conversation/why-has-environmental-documentary-gone-viral-chinas-internet (accessed on March 16, 2015)

Zheng, Yisheng and Qian, Yihong (1998) *Grave Concerns – Problems of Sustainable Development in China [Shendu Youhuan: Dangdai Zhongguo de Kechixu Fazahan Wenti]*. Beijing: Jinri Zhongguo Chubanshe.

Zhou, Yinghua (2002) Report on China's development and investment in land and water. Proceedings of the Regional Consultation. Bangkok, Thailand, October 3–5, 2001. Food and Agriculture Organization of the United Nations Regional Office for Asia and Pacific: Bangkok.

Index